THESE GUYS ARE GOOD™

Published by Senior Tour Wives, Inc.
112 PGA Tour Boulevard
Ponte Vedra Beach, Florida 32082
904-285-3700

Edited, designed, and manufactured
in the United States of America by
Favorite Recipes® Press
an imprint of

FRP™

2451 Atrium Way
Nashville, Tennessee 37214

Art Director: Steve Newman
Designer: David Malone
Project Managers: Jane Hinshaw,
                 Tanis Westbrook
Production Designer: Sara Anglin

Library of Congress Number: 2001-126654
ISBN: 0-9711052-0-0
First Printing: 2002   20,000 copies

THESE GUYS ARE GOOD™

THE SENIOR TOUR WIVES COOKBOOK

Acknowledgements

Cover Art and Design: Peter Max
A very special thank you to Peter Max. Thanks also to Anna, Gene, and Kristen for all of their help. Peter's wonderful donation of the magnificent painting on the cover of our cookbook is extraordinary. What a generous and gifted artist!

Photography: Paul Lester Photography
Many thanks to Paul Lester for the great photos that make our cookbook so special. He was a joy to work with, going above and beyond and doing whatever he had to do to make it work. We appreciate not only his skill with the camera but also the generosity he showed in the donation of his time. Paul, you are the best!

Thanks to Montana Pritchard and Thomas Franklin for the great wives photographs. We appreciate the generous giving of their time and talent.

Special thanks for all the help received in the creating of this wonderful cookbook. Particular thanks to Barbara Nicklaus, Gail Murphy and the people at FRP for all they did to make this book a special one. Thank you for allowing me to chair such a remarkable project.

Susan North, Cookbook Chair

....

The cover art for this book was created by the legendary contemporary artist, Peter Max.

Peter Max and his colorful and imaginative images have become part of the fabric of American pop culture. With his "cosmic art" distinguished by bold linework, blended colors and transcendental themes, Peter Max burst onto the American pop scene in the 1960s and became a household name. Through the '80s and '90s, Max's art  evolved into a new impressionistic style featuring bold, multicolored brushstrokes.

A true patriot, Peter Max has used his canvas to celebrate American icons and symbols. He has painted for the last five U.S. Presidents and has enjoyed a 25-year love affair with Lady Liberty, having immortalized her statue in a series of portraits done annually since the bicentennial. From art that appeared on the first U.S. 10-cent postage stamps to 235 U.S. border murals, Peter Max has captured America at its finest and left an indelible mark on its history.

Internationally, Peter Max has also made his mark. After creating an installment of "Forty Gorbys," he was invited by the former Soviet President to create a museum tour. The premiere of the tour at the Hermitage Museum in St. Petersburg drew the largest attendance for an art opening in Soviet history—almost 15,000 people. Other international works include two giant 155-foot murals for the U.S. Pavilion at the Seville World's Fair; twelve postage stamps for the Earth Summit in Rio de Janeiro; a beautiful sculpture carved from the first piece of the Berlin Wall to reach America; and many others too numerous to mention.

In addition to creating art on behalf of ecology, world peace, and harmony, Peter Max has also had an artistic relationship with the sports world. He has been honored to hold the position of Official Artist for events ranging from five Super Bowls and World Cup USA to the U.S. Open, NYC Marathon, NHL All-Star Game, the World Series 2000, and more.

Max's natural enthusiasm for the blending of fine art with the performing arts can be seen through his involvement with the music and entertainment world. He enjoys special friendships with celebrities the world over, often offering them gifts of their portraits. He has been the Official Artist for five Grammys and recently created a 600- by 80-foot backdrop for Woodstock '99.

His diverse creativity comes from an international upbringing. Max was born in Berlin, spent his earliest years in Shanghai, then moved as a boy to Tibet, Israel, and Paris, finally reaching the United States at age sixteen. Having established his place in America's 20th century pop culture, Max continues to reinvent himself as artist of the new millennium, expanding his fascination with science, technology, and the world of cyberspace.

Whether the nature of Peter Max's gallery is art, media, or virtual, his colors and imagery have made the world a richer and more imaginative place in which to live.

As Albert Einstein said, "Imagination is more important than knowledge."

Contents

• TEE OFF •

Arnold Palmer

• IRONS IN THE FIRE •

Jack Nicklaus

• BIRDIES AND BUNKERS •

Chi Chi Rodriguez

• ON THE GREEN •

Lee Trevino

• THE 19TH HOLE •

Gary Player

Introduction

Senior Tour Wives, Inc., was founded in 1994. Since then, we have raised and donated more than $1.4 million to local charities throughout the United States. Senior Tour Wives, Inc., is dedicated to helping others by donating funds to organizations that aid and benefit women and their families. These charities are located across the United States in our hometowns. We believe that we can make a real difference in the lives of others by helping those organizations in our communities whose objectives and interests are near and dear to our hearts. Proceeds from the sale of this cookbook will enable us to further this mission. Thank you for your support.

All of the recipes in the book were submitted by SENIOR PGA TOUR players and their families. Recipes have not been tested or altered since their submission so that you may enjoy them the way your favorite golfers do in their own homes. We hope you enjoy learning more about these legends of golf through a few of their very own culinary classics and a few not-so-classics, too! Their tastes in the kitchen are as varied as their styles of play on the golf course. Bon appétit!

While compiling this cookbook, we had a wonderful opportunity to reflect on the years we have spent traveling on the Tour. Some of us started traveling a very long time ago, and some of us started as rookies at fifty. You will find many of our stories throughout this book. There are a number of common reflections among those who contributed to the book that we wanted to share as well.

Although the travel that goes along with this life is sometimes the worst part of the job, it is also the best part. The friendships we have made while traveling together are relationships that we will treasure forever. Life on the Tour has changed so much since the early days, but we wouldn't trade those years of struggling and relying on each other for anything. They are priceless. And, despite all of the wonderful places we have been fortunate to visit, home is still the best "vacation" spot around. This journey has been an adventure. We hope you enjoy a few of the great stories from our ride.

FRONT ROW...
Irene Burns
Helen Horton
Wendy Fleisher
Marcia Colbert
Gayle Nelson
Geraldine Morgan

BACK ROW...
Joan Baiocchi
Vivienne Player
Barbara Nicklaus
Hilary Watson
Susan North

FRONT ROW...
Maureen Graham
Angie Quigley
Valerie Jacobs
Tudy Ahern
Pam Tewell
Peggy Gilder

BACK ROW...
Verity Charles
Dell Eastwood
Carol Hall
Kate Doyle
Brenda Albus
Sally McGinnis

FRONT ROW...
Chie Aoki
Esther Fernandez
Gail Murphy

BACK ROW...
Irene Wargo
Carolyn Dougherty
Carolyn Summerhays
Sally Irwin

TEE OFF

APPETIZERS • SOUPS • BREADS

CROSTINI AL FORNO

Gary Player

1 medium onion, chopped
butter
300 grams chicken livers, coarsely chopped
250 milliliters white wine
1 teaspoon cream
1 loaf French bread
1 garlic clove, cut into halves
1 tablespoon olive oil
2 tablespoons olive paste
1 tablespoon napoli sauce or spaghetti sauce
1 ball mozzarella cheese, shredded
1 tablespoon pesto sauce

Sauté the onion in a small amount of butter in a skillet. Add the chicken livers and wine. Simmer until reduced to the desired consistency. Stir in the cream. Cool to room temperature.

Slice the French bread and arrange on a baking sheet. Broil just until lightly toasted. Rub on both sides with the cut side of the garlic and brush with the olive oil.

Spread the olive paste and then the liver mixture on the toasted bread and arrange on the baking sheet. Top with the napoli sauce, mozzarella cheese and pesto sauce. Broil until heated through.

Refer to the Metric Conversion Chart on page 215 for measurement equivalents.

Serves 12

In February of 1977, six tour couples took a week off after the Hawaiian Open and spent it on the island of Kauai. Our daughter Kelly was 10 months old. Dave Marr, our host, organized everything for us right down to the entertainment, which included luaus, tennis tournaments and, of course, sightseeing. Helicopter tours of the island were one of the adventures planned. We wanted to go, but the problem was a babysitter.

"Leave her with me," offered Tom Weiskopf. "I am watching Heidi and Eric while Jeanne plays tennis anyway. It will be fun." We hesitated. Taking care of your own six-year-old is one thing, but adding a baby to the mix is quite another. "Really," piped in Heidi, "it will be great. I'd love to play with a girl for a change."

Off we went for several memorable hours. We returned to find Tom with Kelly on his lap as she happily "played the drums," banging pots and pans with a spoon. This stern competitor who is so legendary for his intensity on the golf course was one of the best "Tour" babysitters Kelly ever had!

FRUIT PIZZA

George Burns

CRUNCHY CRUST	TOPPING
1 1/4 cups flour	15 ounces part-skim ricotta cheese
3/4 cup crushed bran flakes	1 tablespoon sugar
1 tablespoon sugar	1 teaspoon vanilla extract
1 teaspoon baking powder	2 cups sliced strawberries
2/3 cup skim milk	2 medium oranges, peeled, sectioned
1/4 cup vegetable oil	1 kiwifruit, peeled, sliced
	1/2 cup apricot jam (optional)

For the crust, mix the flour, bran flakes, sugar and baking powder in a mixing bowl. Add the skim milk and oil and stir with a fork until the mixture forms a ball. Press into a 14-inch round pizza pan or shallow 10×15-inch baking pan sprayed with nonstick cooking spray or lightly oiled. Bake at 425 degrees for 20 minutes or until golden brown. Let stand until cool or for up to 12 hours.

For the topping, combine the ricotta cheese, sugar and vanilla in a mixing bowl and mix well. Spread evenly over the cooled crust. Arrange the strawberries, oranges and kiwifruit over the cheese mixture. Heat the apricot jam in a small saucepan until melted, stirring constantly. Spoon over the fruit to glaze. Cut into wedges to serve.

You may substitute whole wheat flour for flour, other crushed cereal for the bran flakes or other fruit and berries for the ones suggested.

Serves 8

When we picked out our puppy, who is now 17 years old, I decided to name him Muirfield, after Jack Nicklaus' golf course in Ohio, my home state. When I told Jack that I had named the puppy Muirfield after the course, Jack said that he must be one tough son of a gun. I laughed: our Muirfield is a Bichon Frise, a small white fluffy breed of dog.

PEPPERONI BITES

Mike McCullough

2 cups flour
1 teaspoon garlic powder
1 teaspoon oregano
2 cups milk
2 eggs, beaten
1 cup cubed Muenster cheese
1 cup cubed provolone cheese
2 cups chopped pepperoni

Combine the flour, garlic powder and oregano in a mixing bowl. Add the milk and eggs and mix until smooth. Stir in the Muenster cheese, provolone cheese and pepperoni.

Spread the mixture in a greased 9×13-inch baking pan. Bake at 400 degrees for 30 minutes or until golden brown. Cool to room temperature and cut into squares to serve.

Serves 28

TEE OFF • APPETIZERS • SOUPS • BREADS

Fairly early in my career, I was having "one of those days." It happened at the first tournament that Glen Tait ever officiated. The trouble began when I hit a beautiful drive down the right side of the fairway on the third hole. The marshal was standing in the edge of the fairway, but was not paying attention. My drive hit the marshal squarely on the head (fortunately he was not injured), and ricocheted to the right down a steep embankment and into the tall grass. This was unfamiliar territory for me. I finished the hole with a double bogey, and the day went down hill from there.

A few holes later, one of my drives got stuck in the fork of a branch near the top of a newly planted three-foot-tall pine tree designating the 150-yard mark. I took a baseball swing at the ball toward the green, removing several branches with the motion. I picked up the branches and strategically placed them back in the tree.

After the round, Glen Tait approached me to discuss the tree incident. The president of the club was, understandably, not pleased. Feeling the need to plead my case, I explained that I had been a forestry major at Oklahoma State University (I had actually majored in communications) and, based on my experience, the tree needed a little pruning, so I just took care of it while I was there. Glen laughed, complimented me on my story and fined me $250. On the occasion of his retirement, Glen said it was still the best excuse he had ever heard.

HOT ARTICHOKE DIP

Doug Tewell

1 cup grated Parmesan cheese

1 cup mayonnaise

1 (14-ounce) can plain or marinated artichoke hearts, drained, chopped

2 or 3 dashes Worcestershire sauce (optional)

1 or 2 small garlic cloves, minced (optional)

pepper to taste

Combine the Parmesan cheese, mayonnaise, artichoke hearts, Worcestershire sauce, garlic and pepper in a bowl and mix well. Spoon into a shallow baking dish sprayed with nonstick cooking spray. Bake at 350 degrees until bubbly and golden brown. Serve with thin wheat crackers or other crackers.

Serves 8

I was hitting the ball well, but not scoring like I wanted to, so I called sports psychologist Deborah Graham. We talked for 2¹/₂ hours, during which time I was also writing and cradling the telephone in the crook of my neck. Feeling great mentally, I hung up the telephone, but soon began to feel the physical pain of a pinched nerve in my neck. In adjusting my mental health, I had compromised my physical health. Getting it all together on the SENIOR TOUR is sometimes quite an adventure.

BOGEY-FREE DIP

Bob Duval

1¹/₂ pounds ground beef
1 (8-ounce) jar picante sauce
1 (10-ounce) jar jalapeño peppers, drained
3 tablespoons sour cream
3 cups shredded Cheddar cheese

Brown the ground beef in a skillet, stirring until crumbly; drain. Combine with the picante sauce, jalapeño peppers, sour cream and Cheddar cheese in a serving bowl and mix well. Serve with chips.

Serves 16

TEE OFF • APPETIZERS • SOUPS • BREADS

CHILE SALSA

Arnold Palmer

2 pounds chile peppers
5 pounds tomatoes, peeled, chopped
1 pound onions, chopped
1 cup vinegar
1 tablespoon salt
$1/2$ teaspoon pepper

Cut a slit in the side of each pepper to allow steam to escape. Place on a baking sheet. Roast at 400 degrees for 6 to 8 minutes or until tender: cool to room temperature. Peel the peppers and chop, discarding the seeds.

Combine the tomatoes, peppers, onions, vinegar, salt and pepper in a large saucepan. Bring to a boil and reduce the heat. Simmer for 10 minutes, stirring occasionally. Let cool. Store in an airtight container in the refrigerator.

Remember to wear rubber gloves to prepare chiles.

Makes 12 cups

CURRIED TUNA AND CHUTNEY DIP

Arnold Palmer

1 (7-ounce) can chunk-style tuna, drained
8 ounces cream cheese, softened
3 tablespoons chopped chutney
3 tablespoons milk
1 tablespoon (or more) sherry
$3/4$ teaspoon curry powder

Combine the tuna, cream cheese, chutney, milk, sherry and curry powder in a blender container and process until smooth. Spoon into a serving dish.

Serves 12

Water and sand aren't the only hazards faced on the SENIOR TOUR. Some hazards are behind the scenes. One night, after many weeks of hectic travel and yet another unfamiliar hotel room, I awoke in the middle of the night to answer the call of nature. Unable to locate the light switch, I stumbled into the closet instead of the bathroom. My wife, Tudy, awoke to a terrible racket as I, now entangled in hanging clothes, tried to find my way out. Leaping into action, she turned on the light, and I, even more disoriented by the brightly lit room, jumped back startled and shouted, "Who are you?"

CURRIED VEGETABLE DIP

Jim Ahern

1 cup plain yogurt

1 cup mayonnaise

2 teaspoons soy sauce

2 teaspoons cumin

2 teaspoons curry powder

1 teaspoon garlic powder

1 teaspoon vegetable seasoning

1 teaspoon cayenne pepper

1/4 cup chopped green onions

2 teaspoons chopped fresh parsley or dried parsley

Combine the yogurt, mayonnaise, soy sauce, cumin, curry powder, garlic powder, vegetable seasoning and cayenne pepper in a bowl and mix well.

Stir in the green onions and parsley. Spoon into a serving bowl and serve with fresh vegetables.

Serves 12

TEE OFF • APPETIZERS • SOUPS • BREADS

HOT CRAB COCKTAIL SPREAD

Arnold Palmer

8 ounces cream cheese, softened
1 tablespoon milk
2 teaspoons Worcestershire sauce
2 tablespoons chopped onion
1 (7-ounce) can crab meat, or 8 ounces thawed frozen snow crab meat
2 tablespoons sliced almonds

Combine the cream cheese, milk, Worcestershire sauce and onion in a mixing bowl and mix well. Drain the crab meat and flake into the cream cheese mixture; mix gently.

Spoon into a greased baking dish and top with the almonds. Bake at 350 degrees for 15 minutes. Serve warm with crackers.

Serves 8

MEETING STREET CRAB

Arnold Palmer

1/4 cup (1/2 stick) butter
1/4 cup flour
1 teaspoon salt
1/8 teaspoon pepper
1 cup light cream
1/2 cup sherry
1 pound frozen crab meat, thawed, flaked
3/4 cup shredded Cheddar cheese

Melt the butter in a saucepan and blend in the flour, salt and pepper. Cook until bubbly and stir in the cream and sherry. Cook over low heat until thickened and smooth, stirring constantly.

Remove from the heat and stir in the crab meat. Spoon into a greased baking dish and sprinkle with the cheese. Bake at 425 degrees for 15 minutes or until the cheese melts. Add a salad and crusty bread to serve this as a main dish.

Serves 8

A golfer is allowed to move a loose impediment that is in his putting line. The catch is that it has to be moved with the hand rather than with another object in order to avoid a penalty. So what does a player do when a bird leaves its fresh dropping in his line? He calls over the USGA official with his group and asks him if that is indeed a loose impediment, then asks him to remove it. Without hesitation he will do so with his finger and a coy smile on his face, for he is a member of the USGA.

SHRIMP MOLD

Leonard Thompson

1 envelope unflavored gelatin
1 cup tomato soup
8 ounces cream cheese, softened
2 cups finely chopped shrimp
1 cup chopped celery
1/3 cup chopped onion
1/2 cup chopped green bell pepper
2 tablespoons horseradish

Soften the gelatin in the tomato soup in a mixing bowl. Add the cream cheese and beat until smooth. Stir in the shrimp, celery, onion, green pepper and horseradish.

Spoon the mixture into a lightly oiled mold. Chill for 6 hours or until set. Unmold onto a serving plate and serve with crackers.

Serves 16

TEE OFF • APPETIZERS • SOUPS • BREADS

SALMON MOLD TARTARE

Jerry Heard

16 ounces fresh salmon

1 large shallot, minced

2 tablespoons capers, drained, rinsed

1 tablespoon minced fresh parsley

1 tablespoon minced fresh cilantro

3 tablespoons lemon juice

2 tablespoons spicy mustard

1 tablespoon olive oil

red pepper sauce to taste

salt and pepper to taste

Pulse the salmon in a food processor just until chopped. Combine with the shallot, capers, parsley and cilantro in a bowl and mix gently.

Combine the lemon juice, mustard, olive oil, pepper sauce, salt and pepper in a mixing bowl and mix well. Add to the salmon mixture and toss to mix well.

Spoon the mixture into a lightly oiled mold and chill for 3 hours or longer. Unmold to serve.

Serves 12

Friday night Bible Study

EGGPLANT CAPONATA

....

George Burns

*This recipe for Eggplant Caponata came from Italy with my wife Irene's
great-grandmother and has been handed down and around
to all the women in her family.*

2 large eggplant

$1/2$ cup extra-virgin olive oil

1 cup chopped onion

3 cups drained canned Italian tomatoes

2 tablespoons tomato paste

2 cups chopped celery

3 tablespoons capers

$1/2$ cup Greek olives, pitted, cut into halves

$1/3$ cup balsamic vinegar

$1/4$ cup sugar

salt and pepper to taste

Cut the unpeeled eggplant into $1/2$-inch cubes. Sauté in the heated olive oil
in a large skillet over medium heat for 3 to 4 minutes or until brown. Remove the
eggplant with a slotted spoon to drain.

Add the onion to the drippings in the skillet and sauté until light brown.
Add the tomatoes, tomato paste and celery and mix well. Cook until the celery
is tender. Stir in the capers, olives and eggplant.

Combine the vinegar and sugar in a small saucepan and heat until the sugar
dissolves, stirring frequently. Pour over the eggplant mixture.

Simmer over low heat for 20 minutes, stirring every 5 minutes. Season with
salt and pepper. Spoon into a dish and cool to room temperature before serving.
Serve as a spread on fresh Italian bread or as an accompaniment to a main dish.
Store in an airtight container in the refrigerator.

Serves 6 to 8

At the 2000 Ford Senior Championships, John Bland (Blandie) was not on speaking terms with Brian (Bruno) Henning, the head rules official on the SENIOR TOUR. The cause was some biltong, a South African specialty similar to beef jerky, that Bruno had received. Blandie was upset because Bruno knew of his love for biltong, but hadn't shared it. Blandie confronted Bruno and ended the discussion by saying, "I'm not speaking to you for a few days."

During the tournament, Bland's ball came to rest next to a sprinkler head. When he called for an official to confirm that he had a free drop, he saw that the official approaching was none other than Bruno.

Bruno got out of the cart, Blandie pointed to the ball, and Bruno took a close look, contemplating his decision. He then lifted his arm to indicate his ruling that Bland should drop his ball at the nearest point of relief. The entire ruling was made without a word exchanged—almost. After Blandie took his free drop, Bruno mumbled, "Ball in play," and walked off.

BUTTERNUT SOUP

John Bland

2 medium onions, chopped
30 grams butter
3 cups chicken stock
3 butternut squash, peeled, chopped
1 teaspoon curry powder
nutmeg, salt and pepper to taste
1 cup cream
milk (optional)

Sauté the onions in the heated butter in a large saucepan until tender. Add the chicken stock, squash, curry powder, nutmeg, salt and pepper. Cook, covered, over medium heat until the squash is tender.

Process in the blender in batches and return to the saucepan. Cook until heated through. Add the cream gradually. Stir in a small amount of milk if necessary for the desired consistency.

Refer to the Metric Conversion Chart on page 215 for measurement equivalents.

Serves 6

CHUNKY CHICKEN CHILI

Bob Lunn

1¹/2 cups chopped onions
1 cup chopped green bell pepper
3 jalapeño peppers, chopped, or to taste
2 tablespoons (or less) chili powder
2 teaspoons ground cumin
¹/2 teaspoon dried oregano
2 cups chopped cooked chicken breasts
2 cups chopped cooked chicken thighs
1 cup water
1 (14-ounce) can chicken broth
1 (14-ounce) can stewed tomatoes
1 (12-ounce) bottle reduced-calorie chili sauce
1 tablespoon Worcestershire sauce
1 tablespoon Dijon mustard
¹/2 teaspoon ground red pepper
¹/4 teaspoon black pepper
1 (16-ounce) can Great Northern beans, drained

Spray a heavy saucepan with nonstick cooking spray and heat over medium heat. Add the onions, green pepper and jalapeño peppers. Sauté for 5 minutes. Stir in the chili powder, cumin and oregano. Cook for 2 minutes.

Add the chicken, water, chicken broth, tomatoes, chili sauce, Worcestershire sauce, Dijon mustard, red pepper and black pepper. Bring to a boil and reduce the heat. Simmer, covered, for 20 minutes. Stir in the beans and cook for 5 minutes longer.

Serves 8

TEE OFF • APPETIZERS • SOUPS • BREADS

CHILI

Dave Eichelberger

*My wife says that I have two passions in life: cooking and golf. When I am
not on Tour, I can spend the whole day planning, shopping and creating culinary
masterpieces. This is my version of Texas Poet Laureate J. Frank Dobie's chili.
It is good enough to serve without toppings.*

4 pounds chuck

2 pounds beef suet

1 tablespoon flour

4 cups water or beef broth

4 large tomatoes, peeled, seeded, chopped

1 large yellow onion, chopped

4 to 6 garlic cloves, pressed or minced

2 tablespoons Worcestershire sauce

1/4 cup chili powder

2 tablespoons ground cumin

1 tablespoon ground oregano

1 tablespoon salt

Ask the butcher to coarsely grind the chuck with the 1/8-inch grinding
plate. Sauté the suet in a large saucepan until about 1 cup drippings have been
rendered. Add the ground chuck and cook for 15 minutes or until crumbly and
no longer pink.

Blend the flour with a small amount of the water. Add the flour mixture,
remaining water, tomatoes, onion, garlic, Worcestershire sauce, chili powder,
cumin, oregano and salt to the beef. Simmer, uncovered, for 4 hours, adding
additional water or beef stock as needed for the desired consistency.

Cool to room temperature. Store in the refrigerator overnight. Skim the
congealed grease from the surface and reheat to serve.

Serves 6 to 8

During our early days on the Tour we would stay at hotels with swimming pools so the families could all get together after play was over. We were in Greensboro and the weather was very hot and humid. I was out by the pool, but nothing was working to cool me off, and I was complaining loudly about it. My ingenious wife went to our room and got a water balloon full of ice cold water and broke it over my head! That did quiet me down—for a few seconds.

WINNING CHILI

Jerry McGee

This chili is also good prepared in a slow cooker.

2 medium onions, chopped
1 green bell pepper, chopped
2 pounds lean ground beef
1 (46-ounce) can tomato juice
2 (16-ounce) cans kidney beans, partially drained
1 tablespoon (or more) chili powder
1 teaspoon salt
1/4 teaspoon pepper

Spray a large heavy saucepan with nonstick cooking spray. Add the onions and green pepper and sauté until tender. Add the ground beef and cook until brown and crumbly; drain. Add the tomato juice, kidney beans, chili powder, salt and pepper. Simmer for 1 hour.

Serves 8

Jill McGee tells the following story about her early cooking experiences: Jerry and I were newlyweds in 1973 when we arrived at the Bob Hope Desert Classic and decided to rent a condominium for the week. I was so excited because this meant having some privacy and not worrying about getting dressed for breakfast. In the only other condominium we had rented, I had gone through one dozen eggs before I produced two that were edible. I had also had to call home to find out how to bake a potato. Imagine how panicked I was when Jerry requested chili during the Desert Classic!

Naturally, I called home to get my mother's wonderful chili recipe. Unfortunately, I neglected to ask about the measurement of the chili powder and used the entire one-ounce container in a small pot of chili.

When Jerry and I sat down to eat, he took a spoonful and politely asked if I didn't find it rather hot. And I, being bullheaded and wanting to impress him, responded that it was a bit spicy. I was not about to admit to a cooking error, so my dear husband proceeded to eat his entire serving.

When Jerry returned from his round of golf the following day, he jokingly reported that he had beaten everybody in every group that was 'behind' him that day.

Twenty years later, Jerry says that the kitchen of our next home will be lined with wall-to-wall vending machines. Some things never change!

LEFT TO RIGHT: *Jerry McGee, Tom Kite, Christy O'Connor, Jr.*

At one of my first appearances on the SENIOR TOUR, a spectator noticed the Ford logo on my shirt. He asked me if I was with Ford, and, having a longstanding relationship with Ford Motor Company both through the Tour and my company, Executive Golf, Ltd., I hesitantly responded, "Well . . . yes." The spectator then asked, "Can you come with me?" Curious, I followed the gentleman to the parking lot. Once there, the fellow pointed to the rear of his car and said, "I am getting some kind of rattle coming from my trunk. Can you fix it?" Laughing, I directed the man to his nearest Ford dealer.

CLAM CHOWDER

Jim Ahern

8 slices bacon, cut into 1/4-inch strips

3 large white onions, chopped

1 green bell pepper, chopped

1 (6-ounce) can minced clams

1 (6-ounce) can chopped clams

8 cups milk

4 potatoes, peeled, chopped

2 teaspoons Worcestershire sauce

2 teaspoons Tabasco sauce

1 tablespoon butter

salt and pepper to taste

chopped parsley

Fry the bacon with the onions and green pepper in a large saucepan until the bacon is brown. Add the undrained clams, milk and potatoes. Stir in the Worcestershire sauce, Tabasco sauce, butter, salt and pepper.

Simmer, uncovered, over low heat for 30 minutes or until the potatoes are tender; do not boil. Sprinkle servings with chopped parsley.

Serves 6

TEE OFF • APPETIZERS • SOUPS • BREADS

Nancy Inman reports her launch into the world of techno-golf this way: When Joe went to the qualifying school in November of 1997, I was not very computer literate. Joe told me that all of the scores could be found on PGATOUR.com. Our children took the time to show me all the steps to get on-line and pull up the scores. The next day while they were at school, I actually turned on the computer, accessed America On-Line and pulled up the SENIOR TOUR qualifying scores. The most amazing part was that the first name listed was Joe Inman. My first thought was to wonder how it knew that I wanted to see Joe's scores. Then it dawned on me that Joe was leading the "Q" school at six under par after nine holes. Since he had started in 20th place that day, it is a moment I will never forget.

CORN CHOWDER

Joe Inman, Jr.

1 large potato, peeled, chopped	3 tablespoons flour
1 bay leaf	1¼ cups heavy cream
¼ teaspoon dried sage	kernels from 2 ears fresh corn
½ teaspoon cumin seeds	chopped chives and parsley to taste
2 cups water	¼ teaspoon nutmeg
salt to taste	pepper to taste
1 onion, finely chopped	1½ cups shredded sharp Cheddar cheese
3 tablespoons butter	4 to 5 tablespoons dry white wine

Combine the potato with the bay leaf, sage, cumin, water and salt to taste in a large saucepan. Cook just until the potato is tender. Remove from the heat.

Sauté the onion in the butter in a medium saucepan until tender. Add the flour and mix well. Whisk in the cream.

Add the cream mixture to the undrained potatoes in the large saucepan. Add the corn, chives, parsley and nutmeg. Season with salt and pepper. Simmer for 10 minutes.

Add the cheese and wine and mix well. Cook until the cheese melts, stirring frequently. Remove the bay leaf and adjust the seasonings before serving.

Serves 4 to 6

Our girls grew up in hotels and learned to read hotel signs before they were four years old. They learned to write by signing room service charges. They were accustomed to people asking if I was a player and who I was. I would always tell people that my name was Sam Snead when they asked who I was.

When our youngest was about four years old, she was in an elevator with a baby sitter when the real Sam Snead stepped on. He looked at her and asked if she was a golfer's little girl. She told him that she was Lou Graham's daughter. After a minute, she looked at him and asked, "What's your name?" "Sam Snead," he answered. "No, it's not," she said, "that's what my daddy always says."

SOUTH CAROLINA CRAB SOUP

Lou Graham

Crab Soup is on the menu for the Southern Gourmet Dinner that Patsy Graham prepares for the high bidder in a charity auction.

2 tablespoons chopped onion
2 tablespoons chopped celery
3 tablespoons butter, melted
1 (14-ounce) can chicken broth
salt and red pepper to taste
1½ cups half-and-half
½ cup white wine
12 ounces fresh crab meat

Sauté the onion and celery in the butter in a large saucepan over low heat until tender. Add the chicken broth, salt and red pepper. Bring to a boil and reduce the heat. Simmer for 10 minutes.

Process in a blender until puréed. Return to the saucepan with the half-and-half, wine and crab meat. Cook just until heated through; do not boil.

Serves 6

I became a professional golfer in January of 1954 after winning the San Diego Open as an amateur. In those days, amateurs and pros that had been on the Tour less than six months were not permitted to receive any prize money. I used to tease Dutch Harrison, who received the $2,400 first-prize money that day by asking Dutch if he still had his prize. "I still have mine," I said. I had received a five-piece silver tea service, while the money had gone to the first eligible professional.

COUNTRY SUPPER SOUP

Gene Littler

8 ounces bacon, chopped
2 (10-ounce) cans onion soup
1 (28-ounce) can solid-pack tomatoes
1 cup chopped carrots
1 cup sliced celery
1 cup chopped potato
8 ounces zucchini, chopped
1 garlic clove, minced
1 small bunch parsley, chopped
1 bay leaf, crumbled
thyme, marjoram and basil to taste
salt and pepper to taste
9 cups water
2 cups broken uncooked spaghetti
2 cups cooked dried lima beans and reserved cooking liquid
1/4 cup grated Parmesan cheese

Combine the bacon, onion soup, tomatoes, carrots, celery, potato and zucchini in a large saucepan. Add the garlic, parsley, bay leaf, thyme, marjoram, basil, salt, pepper and water and mix well. Simmer for 1 hour, stirring occasionally.

Add the spaghetti and cook for 30 minutes longer, stirring frequently. Adjust the seasoning and add the lima beans and cooking liquid. Stir in the Parmesan cheese. Cook just until heated through. Serve in heated bowls and pass additional Parmesan cheese.

Serves 8 to 10

I have played golf for so many years, and people have always told me to stop and smell the roses. After years of playing without really noticing my surroundings, I now find myself out in our garden whenever possible. I take photographs of the beautiful flowers and I am so happy that I have taken the advice to stop and smell the roses.

CUCUMBER SOUP

Larry Mowry

Chilled soup is very refreshing on a hot summer day.

2 cucumbers, peeled, seeded
1 garlic clove
1/4 cup chicken broth
1 1/4 cups sour cream
2 teaspoons rice vinegar
chopped tomatoes and chives (optional)

Combine the cucumbers and garlic in a food processor container and process until smooth.

Combine with the chicken broth, sour cream and rice vinegar in a bowl and mix well. Chill for 2 hours or longer. Top servings with chopped tomatoes and chives.

Serves 4 to 6

TEE OFF • APPETIZERS • SOUPS • BREADS

LIME SOUP

....

Jim Ahern

1 white onion, chopped
2 garlic cloves, minced
1 red bell pepper, cut into strips
2 tablespoons vegetable oil
5 (14-ounce) cans chicken broth
2 chicken breasts, cooked, shredded
1 (4-ounce) can chopped green chiles
3 Roma tomatoes, peeled, chopped
2 tablespoons tomato paste
3 tablespoons chopped fresh cilantro
juice of 1 lime
salt and pepper to taste
tortilla chips
shredded Mexican cheeses

Sauté the onion, garlic and red pepper in the vegetable oil in a large saucepan until the onion is translucent. Add the chicken broth, chicken, green chiles, tomatoes, tomato paste, cilantro, lime juice, salt and pepper and mix well. Simmer for 30 minutes.

Sprinkle tortilla chips into serving bowls. Ladle the soup over the chips and top the servings with cheese.

Serves 6 to 8

When I am not traveling on the Tour, I am home representing a country club in the heart of northern California. Our small town is known for its wine and fresh produce. Each season the members of our club, who are local farmers, bring in a variety of produce, including Bing cherries, asparagus, apples, bell peppers, sweet corn, onions, tomatoes, pears, walnuts and fine wines. My wife and I have fun creating dishes based on the season's harvests and send a special thank you to all of the club members who have shared so generously.

SPLIT PEA AND HAM SOUP

Bob Lunn

1 pound dried green split peas

1 pound cooked ham

4 (14-ounce) cans chicken broth

2 onions, chopped

3 large ribs celery, chopped

4 large garlic cloves, chopped

2 teaspoons dried thyme

$1/8$ teaspoon ground cloves

1 large bay leaf

1 cup shredded Gouda cheese

salt and pepper to taste

Combine the peas, ham, chicken broth, onions, celery, garlic, thyme, cloves and bay leaf in a large heavy saucepan. Bring to a boil over high heat. Reduce the heat and simmer, covered, for 1 hour or until the peas are tender, stirring occasionally.

Remove the ham to a plate and cut into bite-size pieces. Return the ham to the saucepan and add the cheese. Simmer until the cheese melts, stirring to mix well. Season with salt and pepper. Discard the bay leaf before serving.

You may add water if needed for the desired consistency.

Serves 6

During the mid-1980s, I taught tax law to graduate accounting students at Texas A&M. My students called me "the absent-minded professor" for a variety of reasons. I went to Baton Rouge to play a mini-tour event in preparation for the SENIOR TOUR. Upon arriving at the site, I found myself the only one there. I had arrived a week early, so I was immediately given the title of "absent-minded golfer."

TACO SOUP

. . . .

Terry Dill

This is an easy soup to make "on Tour" in a limited kitchen.

1 pound ground turkey

1 large onion, chopped

1 envelope taco seasoning mix

1 (14-ounce) can chicken broth

1 (16-ounce) can yellow corn

1 (15-ounce) can ranch-style beans

1 (10-ounce) can tomatoes with green chiles

corn chips (optional)

sour cream (optional)

chopped green onions (optional)

shredded cheese (optional)

avocado slices (optional)

Brown the ground turkey with the onion in a large saucepan sprayed with nonstick cooking spray, stirring until the turkey is crumbly. Stir in the seasoning mix and chicken broth. Add the undrained corn, beans and tomatoes with green chiles and mix well.

Cook until heated through. Top servings with choice of corn chips, sour cream, green onions, shredded cheese and/or avocado slices.

Serves 6

My daughter was graduating from high school in 1996, on the same day as the qualifying day for the U.S. Open. I had chosen to skip both of these events and, as a rookie, had entered the Buick Classic because I thought the Westchester course favored my game. My alarm went off unexpectedly at 2:30 A.M. the morning of the first round. I was very groggy and accidentally reset the alarm for noon. Needless to say, I missed my 10:00 A.M. tee time and was disqualified. The bright side of this story is that I was able to catch a flight home and see my daughter receive her high school diploma.

TURKEY AND RICE SOUP

Allen Doyle

leftover turkey bones
8 cups water
2 cups chopped celery
2 cups chopped carrots
2 cups uncooked instant brown rice
2 tablespoons chicken soup base

Combine the turkey bones with the water in a large saucepan. Simmer for 1 hour. Remove the bones from the broth and cool. Remove the turkey from the bones and discard the bones. Return the turkey to the broth.

Add the celery, carrots, rice and soup base. Bring to a boil and reduce the heat. Simmer for 1 hour longer.

Serves 8

TEE OFF • APPETIZERS • SOUPS • BREADS

In 1970 after finishing play in Napa, California, Sally and I set out for Boulder, Colorado, driving as far as Salt Lake City the first night. Severe winter storm warnings were on the television the next morning, but it looked as if the storm was not headed in our direction. We drove all day and stopped for dinner in Cheyenne. We ate quickly, as the snow storm was closing in, and bad weather was on our heels. Deciding to try to outrun the storm will not go down as one of my better ideas. The storm soon escalated into a blizzard with whiteout conditions, blowing snow, no visibility and no towns in sight. We were scared but dared not stop. Suddenly, as we were inching our way down the road, a snow plow came from behind and we were able to follow it out of the blizzard and were soon on our way to Boulder. Sally and I enjoyed our car trips together in those days, but we are very happy today to fly to most of our destinations.

BANANA BREAD

Hale Irwin

2 eggs
1/2 cup (1 stick) butter, melted, cooled
1 cup sugar
1 cup mashed ripe bananas
1 tablespoon vanilla extract
2 cups flour
1 1/2 teaspoons baking powder
1 1/2 teaspoons baking soda
1/2 teaspoon salt
3/4 cup buttermilk
3/4 cup chopped pecans

Beat the eggs in a mixing bowl. Add the butter, sugar, bananas and vanilla and mix well. Mix the flour, baking powder, baking soda and salt together. Add to the banana mixture and mix just until moistened. Stir in the buttermilk and pecans.

Spoon into a buttered 5×9-inch loaf pan. Bake at 325 degrees for 1 hour and 5 minutes or until the bread begins to pull away from the sides of the pan. Cool in the pan on a wire rack for 10 minutes. Loosen the loaf from the pan with a knife and remove to the wire rack to cool completely.

Makes 1 loaf

There are two ways to pack a suitcase on Tour. The player packs his suitcase week after week and develops a method: pants first, then shirts and sweaters, next socks and underwear, etc. The order never changes. On the other hand, the suitcase of the accompanying partner is never quite so neat. Her idea of packing is to cram in as much as she can and then to have to go shopping for the necessary items left at home. Funny how that works.

GRAMMY'S BANANA BREAD

Gil Morgan

BREADS • SOUPS • APPETIZERS • TEE OFF

1/2 cup (1 stick) margarine, softened

1 cup sugar

2 eggs

2 cups flour

1 teaspoon baking soda

2 or 3 ripe bananas, mashed

2 tablespoons orange juice

1/2 cup chopped pecans

Cream the margarine and sugar in a mixing bowl until light and fluffy. Beat in the eggs. Add the flour and baking soda and mix well. Beat in the bananas and orange juice. Add the pecans and mix by hand.

Spoon into a greased 5×9-inch loaf pan. Bake at 350 degrees for 1 hour or until a wooden pick inserted into the center comes out clean. Remove to a wire rack to cool.

Makes 1 loaf

The Big Island of Hawaii is a place we love to visit as a family every year. My wife grew up there and that's where we were married, so we have many happy memories of this special spot. When DC was a child, her family would go to the Kona Inn for breakfast every Sunday morning after going to the old Hawaiian Church across the street. The banana bread was a staple at breakfast or lunch, and it is as no-fail as you can get. For some reason, this tastes just great with my chili (page 25).

KONA INN BANANA BREAD

Dave Eichelberger

Banana bread is a great way to use up overripe bananas, but do not substitute margarine for the butter in this recipe.

2 1/2 cups cake flour
2 teaspoons baking powder
1 teaspoon salt
1 cup (2 sticks) butter, softened
2 cups sugar
6 ripe bananas, mashed (about 3 cups)
4 eggs, beaten

Sift the cake flour, baking powder and salt together 3 times. Cream the butter and sugar in a mixing bowl until light and fluffy. Add the bananas and eggs and beat until smooth. Add the flour mixture and mix well.

Spoon into 2 lightly oiled 5×9-inch loaf pans. Bake at 350 degrees for 45 to 60 minutes or until the loaves are firm in the center and the edges pull away from the sides of the pans. Remove to wire racks to cool.

Makes 2 loaves

In the early days of the regular Tour, there were qualifying matches on Mondays to earn spots to play every week. We were a group of friends traveling the country like a community of gypsies. Income was low, and the nonexempt players stuck together for encouragement, staying in the same cheap hotels and eating together. It was not very grand or glorious, but it surely was fun.

IRISH TREACLE BREAD

Jim Albus

Our son Mark is now the family treacle bread maker, using a recipe that was brought from Ireland by my grandmother.

2 cups flour
$1/2$ teaspoon baking powder
$1/2$ teaspoon baking soda
$1/2$ teaspoon salt
$1/2$ cup dark molasses
$1/2$ cup buttermilk

Mix the flour, baking powder, baking soda and salt in a mixing bowl. Add the molasses and buttermilk and mix to form a dough. Knead the dough briefly on a surface sprinkled generously with flour. Shape into a square $1/2$ inch thick.

Cut the square into quarters. Bake on an unoiled griddle or electric skillet set at 325 degrees for 5 minutes on each side. Test for doneness by cutting horizontally into the middle of 1 square.

Slice as for an English muffin to serve. Toast the halves for a crisper version.

Serves 4

Lynette Coody remembers an incident when Charles won the Masters in 1971. She had packed lightly, not expecting the victory, and did not bring a dress to wear to the Champions Dinner. It was Sunday and everything was closed, so she borrowed a black dress from one friend and a beautiful diamond pin from another, but no one had shoes that she could borrow. She had to attend this very special dinner in the only shoes she had brought—white. She said that, being from the South, she was certain that it was not the proper look, but she was not about to stay home!

JALAPENO CORN BREAD

Charles Coody

1 cup yellow cornmeal

1 (20-ounce) can cream-style yellow corn

1 cup shredded Cheddar cheese

1 medium onion, chopped

3 medium garlic cloves, chopped

1 (4-ounce) can chopped jalapeño peppers, drained

1 tablespoon baking powder

1 teaspoon salt

2 eggs

1 cup sour cream

2/3 cup vegetable oil

butter

Combine the cornmeal, corn, cheese, onion, garlic, jalapeño peppers, baking powder and salt in a bowl. Add the eggs, sour cream and vegetable oil and mix well.

Melt enough butter in a 9×13-inch baking pan to cover the bottom of the pan. Spoon the batter into the pan. Bake at 350 degrees for 50 to 60 minutes or until golden brown and set.

You may substitute 1/2 to 1 small can of chopped green chiles for the jalapeño peppers for a milder version.

Serves 12

MONKEY BREAD

....

Larry Nelson

*Monkey bread is a family favorite and is expected to be found
on our table every Christmas.*

4 cans Butter-Me-Not refrigerator biscuits
3/4 cup sugar
1 tablespoon cinnamon
3/4 cup (1 1/2 sticks) butter
1 cup sugar
1 tablespoon cinnamon

Cut each biscuit into quarters. Mix 3/4 cup sugar and 1 tablespoon cinnamon in a sealable container. Add the biscuits and shake to coat well. Arrange in a buttered 10-inch tube pan.

Combine the butter, 1 cup sugar and 1 tablespoon cinnamon in a saucepan. Cook over low heat until the butter melts, stirring frequently. Pour evenly over the biscuits.

Bake at 350 degrees for 40 minutes, covering with foil during the last 15 minutes to prevent overbrowning. Let stand for 5 minutes. Invert onto a serving plate. Pull apart to serve.

Serves 8

TEE OFF • APPETIZERS • SOUPS • BREADS

I was so excited about playing in the Par Three contest during my first Masters, but when I arrived at Augusta National to get ready to compete and opened the trunk to get my clubs, I found it empty! I had forgotten to put the clubs in the car and had to make a mad dash back to my rental house to get my clubs.

I played with Homero Blancas at the Masters one year. At the 18th hole Homero pushed his shot and the ball happened to lodge itself in a woman's bra. Homero called me over and asked, "What should I do?" I replied, "Play it." So I picked the ball out of the woman's bra and handed it to Homero. Naturally, he had a free drop out of the bra. I laughed and told him that if it had been my ball, I would have played it where it landed.

MANGO BREAD

Chi Chi Rodriguez

4 cups flour

3 cups sugar

4 teaspoons baking soda

4 teaspoons cinnamon

1 teaspoon salt

2 cups vegetable oil

6 eggs

2 teaspoons vanilla extract

4 cups chopped mangoes

1 cup raisins

1/2 cup chopped nuts

Sift the flour, sugar, baking soda, cinnamon and salt into a large mixing bowl; make a well in the center. Pour the vegetable oil, eggs and vanilla into the well and mix well. Stir in the mangoes, raisins and nuts.

Spoon into 2 greased loaf pans. Bake at 350 degrees for 1 hour. Remove to a wire rack to cool.

Makes 2 loaves

TEE OFF • APPETIZERS • SOUPS • BREADS

Over the years, I met and played golf with many celebrities. Once at a Pro-Am party, I introduced Joe DiMaggio to our eight-year-old daughter Debbie and asked, "Do you know who this is?" She smiled and answered, "Yes, he's Mr. Coffee." I said, "No, Deb, he's Mr. Baseball."

Our children grew up on the Tour in the days when port-a-cribs were not plentiful at the hotels where we stayed. We usually traveled with our own, which collapsed and fit perfectly along the driver's side from front to back. The only problem was that the driver had to enter the car on the passenger side.

PUMPKIN BREAD

Jim Colbert

4 eggs

1 cup canola oil

2/3 cup water

1 (16-ounce) can pumpkin

3 1/2 cups flour

3 cups sugar

2 teaspoons baking soda

4 to 5 teaspoons pumpkin pie spice

2 to 3 teaspoons cinnamon

2 teaspoons salt

Beat the eggs in a mixing bowl. Add the canola oil, water and pumpkin and mix well. Mix the flour, sugar, baking soda, pumpkin pie spice, cinnamon and salt in a bowl. Add to the pumpkin mixture 1 cup at a time, mixing well after each addition.

Spoon into a greased bundt pan. Bake at 350 degrees for 1 hour or until a wooden pick comes out clean. Cool on a wire rack. Store in the refrigerator or freezer.

You may bake in 3 medium loaf pans if preferred.

Serves 18

When the golfers first joined the Tour, we usually drove from tournament to tournament. One golfer had been traveling for the first part of the year with his dog and daughter. After a day on the golf course, the golfer came home to find his wife, his daughter and the dog on the swing set. As he approached, his wife said, "Pick two, any two. I don't care which two, but I'm telling you that after this week only two of us will be traveling." The choice was made and they really missed their daughter. Just kidding— they found the dog a new home and they all lived happily ever after.

ORANGE ZUCCHINI BREAD
....

Allen Doyle

^{1}/2 cup vegetable oil

1 cup sugar

2 eggs

^{1}/2 cup thawed frozen orange juice concentrate

2 teaspoons vanilla extract

1^1/2 cups flour

^{1}/4 teaspoon baking powder

^{1}/2 teaspoon salt

1 cup chopped walnuts

2 cups shredded zucchini

Combine the vegetable oil, sugar, eggs, orange juice concentrate and vanilla in a mixing bowl and mix well. Add the flour, baking powder and salt and mix until smooth. Stir in the walnuts and zucchini.

Spoon into a greased and floured 5×9-inch loaf pan. Bake at 350 degrees for 1^1/4 hours. Remove to a wire rack to cool.

Makes 1 loaf

In 1979 Sally and I had a fabulous week at the South African PGA, including winning the tournament and visiting Gary and Vivienne Player's farm. We had also arranged for a three-day holiday with Dave and Cathy Stockton following the tournament. It turned out to be a series of adventures. We had been assured that we would not be going to the game park in which a woman had recently been trampled to death, but as the plane was landing and the Range Rover was clearing the wild animals from the runway, we discovered that we were, indeed, at that game park. We were greeted in camp by a shot fired to kill a spitting cobra in the lunch area. Each night got longer and longer as the power for the lights came from a generator that was running low. We began to wish that the fence ran all the way around the camp rather than just in front. The jumbo elephant we spotted was not too happy about us and mock charged, sending Sally under her seat. We were happy to start home, but on our way back to Johannesburg, we had to land in Rhodesia, flying at low altitude and without lights for 30 minutes at landing and take-off to avoid heat-seeking missiles. All in all, it was an exciting trip to South Africa, a country we have come to love.

ZUCCHINI BREAD

....

Hale Irwin

3 eggs

1 cup vegetable oil

2 cups sugar

1 tablespoon vanilla extract

3 cups sifted flour

1/4 teaspoon baking powder

1 teaspoon baking soda

1 tablespoon cinnamon

1 teaspoon salt

2 cups shredded peeled zucchini

1/2 cup chopped walnuts

Combine the eggs, vegetable oil, sugar and vanilla in a mixing bowl and beat until smooth. Sift the flour, baking powder, baking soda, cinnamon and salt together. Add to the egg mixture and mix well. Fold in the zucchini and walnuts.

Spoon into 2 greased and waxed paper-lined 5×9-inch loaf pans. Bake at 325 degrees for 1 hour or until the loaves test done.

Makes 2 loaves

IRONS
IN THE
FIRE

• MEATS •

There was a rain delay during the PGA at West Palm Beach in Florida. Jack Nicklaus and Bob Murphy were in a buffet line when a man began banging on the window while pointing and calling to Jack. Always the gentleman, Jack said to Bob, "I'd better sign this autograph." When Jack opened the door, the man asked, "Is Arnie in there?"

MARINATED FLANK STEAK

Jack Nicklaus

^{1}/2 cup vegetable oil

^{1}/3 cup dry burgundy

^{1}/4 cup soy sauce

2 teaspoons red wine vinegar

3 tablespoons minced green onions with tops

1 or 2 tablespoons brown sugar

1 teaspoon dry mustard

^{1}/2 teaspoon basil

^{1}/8 teaspoon marjoram

^{1}/4 teaspoon pepper

1 (1^1/2-pound) flank steak

Combine the vegetable oil, wine, soy sauce and vinegar in a sealable plastic bag or bowl with a tight-fitting lid. Add the green onions, brown sugar, dry mustard, basil, marjoram and pepper and mix well for the marinade.

Add the steak to the marinade and mix to coat well. Marinate in the refrigerator for 8 hours or longer; drain.

Grill over hot coals for 5 minutes on each side or until done to taste. Cut into thin diagonal slices to serve.

You may also broil the steak if preferred.

Serves 4

IRONS IN THE FIRE • MEATS

Patsy Graham tells the following story about Sam Snead: During the 70s Lou and Sam had the same manager, so we traveled to a number of tournaments around the country with him. He would always tell me that if I would just drop the "old man" we could run away together. When our daughter was in college, she joined us at the Disney World Tournament. Sam happened to be playing that week, so I took our daughter over to meet him. The first thing he said to her was, "Boy, if I wasn't married we could run away together." I reminded him that he had always promised that he would run away with me. He looked me straight in the eye and said, "What would I want with a Model-T when there is a Cadillac in the driveway?" Whenever I begin to feel a little haughty, I always remember that I have been compared to a Model-T.

TENNESSEE TENDERLOIN

Lou Graham

This is delicious served cold at a cocktail party.

1 (3- to 4-pound) beef tenderloin, trimmed
garlic powder and freshly ground pepper to taste
2 3/4 cups soy sauce
3/4 cup Jack Daniel's bourbon

Wipe the tenderloin dry with a paper towel and rub with garlic powder and pepper. Combine the soy sauce and bourbon in a large sealable plastic bag. Add the tenderloin and mix to coat well. Marinate at room temperature for 2 hours or in the refrigerator for 8 hours or longer; drain.

Place the tenderloin in a roasting pan. Place in a 450-degree oven and reduce the temperature to 400 degrees. Roast for 40 to 50 minutes for rare. Slice to serve.

Serves 8 to 12

These helpful tips come from my own experiences while grilling. Enjoy.

Don't use gasoline to start your charcoal unless you don't need your eyebrows.

Do use a hairdryer to speed up the heating time for charcoal if you're in a hurry to watch golf on TV. Suggestion: Don't use your wife's hairdryer.

It's extremely difficult to start wet charcoal even with a hairdryer.

If you use only one barbecue mitt, make sure it's on the hand that lifts the hot grill when tossing in the smoking chips.

If you want a hot fire make sure the vents are open.

Don't forget that old food and grill rust are necessary condiments for a pure barbecue flavor!

SIMPLY STEAK KANSAS CITY STYLE

Tom Watson

1 large handful of mesquite wood chips
1 (1-inch-thick) steak
seasoned salt and finely ground pepper to taste

Soak the wood chips in water for at least 2 hours. Sprinkle the steak generously with seasoned salt and pepper and rub in the seasonings.

Drain the mesquite chips and add to the hot coals just before grilling. Grill the steak, covered, for 8 minutes, turning after 3 minutes for medium-rare. Test for doneness by finger pressure.

Use half the amount of mesquite chips to grill fish. Grill one-inch pork chops for 5 minutes on each side; grill one-inch lamb chops for 4 minutes, turning after 3 minutes. Grill chicken bone side down over indirect heat for about 1 hour, turning after 20 minutes on the first side and turning back after 10 minutes on the second side.

Serves 1 or 2

During the 2000 US Open at Pebble Beach, my wife, Hilary, and I went to dinner at Spanish Bay with Jack, Barbara, Jackie and Steve Nicklaus and Andy, Susan and Andrea North. As dessert is always a "must" with this group, we put in our dessert orders and Jack went off to catch the last minute of an important basketball game. When his ice cream came, it was as hard as a rock. I asked the waiter to put it in the microwave for a few seconds, but it came back very, very soft. I said to everyone at the table, "I bet he won't even notice that his ice cream is melted and will eat it all." We all laughed as Jack sat down to his melted ice cream and, without even paying attention, finished the entire bowl—proving that I do know "Jack."

BEEF BURGUNDY

Bob Gilder

1/2 cup flour

1/2 teaspoon salt

1/8 teaspoon pepper

3 pounds stew beef, cut into
2-inch cubes

2 tablespoons olive oil

3 tablespoons butter

1/4 cup brandy

3 slices bacon, chopped

2 cups chopped onions

2 garlic cloves, minced

3/4 cup thinly sliced carrots

3 cups burgundy

2 cups beef bouillon

2 tablespoons minced parsley

1 bay leaf

1/2 teaspoon thyme

12 pearl onions

1 teaspoon sugar

2 tablespoons butter

24 firm white mushroom caps

1 tablespoon butter

Mix the flour with the salt and pepper in a plastic bag. Add the beef and shake to coat well. Heat the olive oil with 3 tablespoons butter in a skillet. Add the beef and cook until brown on all sides. Remove the beef to a baking dish with a slotted spoon, reserving the drippings in the skillet.

Warm the brandy in a small saucepan. Ignite the brandy and pour over the beef.

Add the bacon to the skillet and sauté until partially cooked. Add the chopped onions, garlic and carrots and sauté until tender. Add the sautéed vegetables and bacon to the baking dish with the wine, bouillon, parsley, bay leaf and thyme.

Bake, covered, at 325 degrees for 2 hours. Sauté the pearl onions with the sugar in 2 tablespoons butter in a small skillet until light brown. Add to the baking dish with additional liquid if needed for the desired consistency. Bake for 1 hour longer.

Sauté the mushrooms in 1 tablespoon butter in a small skillet. Add to the baking dish during the last 5 minutes of baking time. Discard the bay leaf. Serve immediately or cool and store in the refrigerator to reheat up to 2 days later.

Serves 8

While they were at a tournament party in Palm Springs, Arnold Palmer and Jack Nicklaus decided to dance! As a woman passed by their table, her blonde wig fell off. Jack picked it up and put it on Arnold and asked him to dance, but Arnold put the wig on Jack's head and led him across the dance floor.

MARINATED BEEF TENDERLOIN

Arnold Palmer

1/2 cup each red wine and chili sauce	1 teaspoon Worcestershire sauce
1/4 cup vegetable oil	1 bay leaf
3 tablespoons wine vinegar	salt and pepper to taste
1 tablespoon chopped onion	1 (4-pound) beef tenderloin

Combine the wine, chili sauce, vegetable oil, vinegar, onion, Worcestershire sauce, bay leaf, salt and pepper in a shallow dish. Add the tenderloin, turning to coat well. Marinate in the refrigerator for several hours; drain. Place the tenderloin in a roasting pan and insert a meat thermometer into the thickest portion. Place in a 500-degree oven. Reduce the temperature to 350 degrees and roast to 120 degrees on the meat thermometer for rare or until done to taste.

Serves 12

BEEF BURGUNDY AND NOODLES

David Lundstrom

1^1/$_2$ pounds mushrooms

3 tablespoons butter

1 tablespoon vegetable oil

3 pounds steak, cut into cubes

^{2}/$_3$ cup beef bouillon

^{3}/$_4$ cup burgundy

2 tablespoons soy sauce

^{1}/$_2$ small onion, grated

1 garlic clove, minced

2 tablespoons cornstarch

^{1}/$_3$ cup beef bouillon

^{1}/$_2$ (10-ounce) can cream of mushroom soup

hot cooked noodles

Sauté the mushrooms in 1^1/$_2$ tablespoons of the butter in a skillet until tender. Place in a deep baking dish. Add the remaining 1^1/$_2$ tablespoons butter and vegetable oil to the skillet. Add the beef and cook until brown on all sides. Remove to the baking dish.

Pour ^{2}/$_3$ cup beef bouillon into the skillet and stir to deglaze the skillet. Add the wine, soy sauce, onion and garlic. Dissolve the cornstarch in ^{1}/$_3$ cup beef bouillon in a small cup. Stir into the wine mixture in the skillet. Cook over low heat until thickened, stirring constantly. Pour over the beef and mushrooms in the baking dish.

Bake, covered, at 275 degrees for 1 hour. Stir in the mushroom soup just before serving. Serve over noodles.

Serves 4 to 6

I was down to my last pair of pants while on Tour. I showered and put on my pants only to discover that they were not my pants and were much too short, even on me! The dry cleaners had given me the wrong pair of pants and someone else had mine. The problem was, however, I had no idea in which city these pants had been cleaned.

GAME DAY STEW

Bruce Summerhays

Stew in the slow cooker is great for golf days because it can be put together early in the day and left to cook without watching. We sneak other healthy vegetables such as peas, corn, turnips and Brussels sprouts into this stew and the kids don't know it.

1¹/₂ pounds stew beef, cubed

5 medium potatoes, chopped

3 cups chopped carrots

1 (10-ounce) can cream of mushroom soup

1 (10-ounce) can cream of chicken soup

1 envelope onion soup mix

2 cups water

pepper to taste

1 cup chopped vegetables of choice (optional)

Combine the beef, potatoes, carrots, canned soups, soup mix, water and pepper in a slow cooker. Add other vegetables as desired. Cook on Low for 6 hours or longer.

You may sear the beef before adding to the slow cooker if preferred.

Serves 6

LIVERPOOL SCOUSE

John Morgan

Scouse, a kind of stew, rhymes with house. It is good on a cold evening.

2 medium onions, chopped
2 tablespoons olive oil
1¹/2 pounds stew beef
pepper to taste
3 bay leaves
3 cups beef stock
2 carrots, peeled, chopped
2 parsnips, peeled, chopped
4 or 5 large potatoes, peeled, cut into quarters
2 teaspoons flour
¹/2 cup water

Sauté the onions in the heated olive oil in a saucepan. Add the beef and cook for 2 to 3 minutes or until brown; drain. Sprinkle with pepper and add the bay leaves and half the beef stock. Simmer for 1 hour.

Add the remaining beef stock, carrots, parsnips and potatoes. Simmer for 45 minutes. Blend the flour with the water in a small cup. Add to the saucepan. Simmer for 15 minutes longer, stirring frequently. Discard the bay leaves before serving.

Serves 4 or 5

MEATS • IRONS IN THE FIRE

We had a tradition when our girls were little. When I left for the golf course, the girls would say, "Play well, Daddy. No bogeys and no three-putts, only birdies and eagles." Once when Erica was almost three years old, she said, "Play well, Daddy. No bogeys and no three-putts. Only beagles."

ENCHILADAS

Ed Sneed

ENCHILADA SAUCE

2 each carrots and ribs celery, minced

1 small onion, chopped

1 bay leaf

1 teaspoon oregano

1 tablespoon crumbled crisp-fried bacon

2 tablespoons butter

Madeira

1/4 cup bacon drippings

1/4 cup flour

1 (8-ounce) can tomato purée

2 tablespoons each parsley and chili powder

10 whole peppercorns

3 beef bouillon cubes

8 cups water

ENCHILADAS

tortillas

vegetable oil

shredded cooked chicken or beef

chopped onion

shredded Cheddar cheese

guacamole

salsa

sour cream

chopped scallions

For the sauce, sauté the carrots, celery, onion, bay leaf, oregano and bacon in the butter in a skillet for 20 minutes or until tender. Add enough wine to deglaze the skillet, stirring to remove browned bits from the skillet. Heat the bacon drippings in a heavy saucepan over high heat. Add the flour and cook until the flour is brown, stirring constantly to prevent overbrowning. Stir in the sautéed vegetables, tomato purée, parsley, chili powder and peppercorns. Add the bouillon cubes and water gradually, stirring constantly. Bring to a boil and reduce the heat. Simmer for 2 to 3 hours or until the sauce is reduced to the consistency of heavy cream. Discard the bay leaf. Cool the mixture slightly. Process in batches in a food processor until smooth. Season with salt and pepper.

For the enchiladas, soften tortillas in heated oil in a skillet. Fill with chicken or beef, onion and cheese. Roll the tortillas to enclose the filling and arrange seam side down in a baking dish. Top with the sauce. Bake at 350 degrees until heated through. Top with additional sauce and cheese, guacamole, salsa, sour cream and/or chopped scallions.

Serves 8

BRAISED OXTAIL

John Bland

15 small pieces of oxtail
2 tablespoons vegetable oil
4 potatoes, peeled, cut into halves
2 carrots, chopped
1 onion, chopped
2 tablespoons vegetable oil
8 ounces sliced mushrooms
2 tablespoons flour
3 cups beef stock
1 cup red wine
2 tablespoons Worcestershire sauce

Brown the oxtail in small batches in 2 tablespoons vegetable oil in a skillet, removing the browned pieces to a baking dish with a slotted spoon. Add the potatoes to the baking dish.

Sauté the carrots and onion in 2 tablespoons vegetable oil in the skillet. Add to the baking dish. Add the mushrooms to the drippings in the skillet and cook over medium heat for 4 minutes. Stir in the flour. Reduce the heat and cook for several minutes, stirring constantly.

Stir in the beef stock and wine. Bring to a boil and cook until thickened, stirring constantly. Stir in the Worcestershire sauce. Add to the baking dish and mix gently.

Bake, covered, at 350 degrees for 1 1/2 hours. Bake, uncovered, for 30 minutes longer. Serve over rice or mashed potatoes.

Serves 6

I was playing in the Irish Open, and we were in a courtesy car on the way to the golf course when we had to stop at a railroad crossing to wait for a train. While we were stopped there, we were hit from behind by another car. The driver of the courtesy car didn't want to make me late for my tee time, so she asked if they could just exchange information and get together later. They asked a man who was walking his dog to be their witness. He tied his dog to the train barrier in order to sign the paper, but just then the train went by, and the barrier went up—dog and all. They got the dog down safely and all was well.

CORNED BEEF AND CABBAGE

Christy O'Connor, Jr.

2 whole onions, peeled

whole cloves

1 (4-pound) corned beef

1 large carrot, sliced

1 teaspoon dry mustard

1 bunch thyme

1 bunch parsley

1 head cabbage, quartered

salt and pepper to taste

12 potatoes, peeled, cooked, halved

Stud 1 of the onions with cloves. Combine the corned beef with the carrot, onions, dry mustard, thyme and parsley in a large saucepan. Add water to cover. Bring to a boil and skim the surface of the water. Simmer, covered, for 45 minutes.

Add the cabbage, salt and pepper. Simmer, covered, for 2 hours longer. Remove and slice the beef. Drain the vegetables, discarding the herbs and reserving the stock for another use. Serve the beef with the cabbage mixture and the potatoes.

Use the stock as a soup base or as the liquid to cook dried split yellow or green peas.

Serves 4

PASTA BOLOGNESE

Dana Quigley

I love Pasta Bolognese and Angie usually makes it for me every ten days or so.
When we are traveling, she usually modifies the sauce with commercial
spaghetti meat sauce instead of the canned tomatoes, and whatever
other ingredients are on hand.

1 large carrot, chopped
1 large rib celery, chopped
8 ounces pancetta or bacon, chopped
2 tablespoons butter
10 ounces lean ground beef
2 hot or sweet Italian sausages, casings removed
salt and pepper to taste
1/2 cup dry white wine
2 (14-ounce) cans crushed Italian plum tomatoes
1 (10-ounce) can beef broth
hot cooked pasta
grated Parmesan cheese

Sauté the carrot, celery and pancetta in the butter in a saucepan for 10 to 15 minutes or until the vegetables are tender.

Brown the ground beef and sausages in a skillet, stirring until crumbly; drain. Season with salt and pepper. Add the wine and simmer for 5 minutes.

Stir in the tomatoes, beef broth and sautéed vegetables and pancetta. Reduce the heat and simmer, loosely covered, for 2 hours, stirring occasionally.

Serve over hot cooked pasta and top with grated Parmesan cheese. Serve with a green vegetable and salad.

Serves 6

IRONS IN THE FIRE • MEATS

Dana lives in a house that his wife bought without his ever having seen it. During the summer of 1998, a friend told Angie of a house that she thought they would like for sale in West Palm Beach.

They were only in their second year on the Tour and had not thought of buying a house, but Angie called the realtor and after receiving the faxed material, decided to see the house. She flew to West Palm Beach, looked at the house, and decided they had to have it. Dana didn't have time to see it, but told her to make an offer. She made the offer and set the closing date without Dana ever seeing the house.

Dana's friends on the Tour teased him about buying a house he had never seen, but he would respond, "Angie likes it, so it's okay with me." He won the Emerald Coast Classic on Sunday, flew to West Palm Beach that evening, saw the house on Monday and closed the deal on Thursday. "Of course," Angie says, "he loved the house."

Dana and Angie Quigley

CONFETTI SPAGHETTI

Miller Barber

12 ounces uncooked spaghetti

1 1/2 pounds ground beef

1 medium green bell pepper, chopped

1 medium onion, chopped

1 (14-ounce) can diced tomatoes

1 (8-ounce) can tomato sauce

1 tablespoon brown sugar

1 teaspoon chili powder

1/4 teaspoon garlic powder

1 teaspoon salt

1/4 teaspoon cayenne pepper

1/2 teaspoon black pepper

3/4 cup shredded Cheddar cheese

Cook the spaghetti using the package directions; drain.

Brown the ground beef with the green pepper and onion in a large skillet over medium heat, stirring until crumbly; drain. Stir in the undrained tomatoes, tomato sauce, brown sugar, chili powder, garlic powder, salt, cayenne pepper and black pepper.

Add the spaghetti to the beef mixture and mix well. Spoon into a greased 9×13-inch baking dish.

Bake, covered, at 350 degrees for 30 minutes. Sprinkle with the cheese and bake, uncovered, for 5 minutes longer or until the cheese melts.

Serves 12

IRONS IN THE FIRE • MEATS

MEXICAN CORN BREAD CASSEROLE

Gil Morgan

CASSEROLE
1 pound ground beef

1 large onion, chopped

1 (28-ounce) can diced tomatoes

1 (4-ounce) can chopped green chiles

4 teaspoons chili powder

1$^{1/2}$ teaspoons sugar

1$^{1/2}$ teaspoons salt

1 (16-ounce) can pinto beans

1 cup shredded cheese

CORN BREAD TOPPING
1 cup cornmeal

$^{1/2}$ teaspoon baking soda

1 (16-ounce) can cream-style corn

1 cup milk

2 eggs

salt and pepper to taste

For the casserole, brown the ground beef with the onion in a skillet, stirring until crumbly; drain. Add the undrained tomatoes, green chiles, chili powder, sugar and salt and mix well. Simmer for 15 minutes. Stir in the beans. Spoon into a deep 9×11-inch baking dish. Sprinkle with the cheese.

For the topping, combine the cornmeal, baking soda, corn, milk, eggs, salt and pepper in a bowl and mix well. Spoon over the ground beef mixture. Bake at 350 degrees for 45 minutes or until the topping is golden brown.

Serves 4

My wife Norma has a theory as to why there are ropes separating the players from the gallery. A few weeks after our September wedding in 1963, I was playing in a tournament in Las Vegas. I was in good standing on Sunday, although on a particular hole, I hit my ball into the bunker. Just before I went into the bunker, she tapped me on the shoulder and asked me for a quarter for the ice cream man. I said, "Now?" And she said, "Of course, now. Otherwise the ice cream man will be gone!"

FAVORITE MEAT LOAF

Al Kelley

1 (8-ounce) can tomato sauce

1/4 cup packed brown sugar

1 tablespoon prepared mustard

2 pounds lean ground beef

2 eggs, lightly beaten

1 medium onion, chopped

1 cup bread crumbs

2 tablespoons Worcestershire sauce

Mix the tomato sauce, brown sugar and mustard in a small bowl. Combine half the mixture with the ground beef, eggs, onion, bread crumbs and Worcestershire sauce in a large mixing bowl and mix well.

Place in a 2-quart baking dish and top with the remaining tomato sauce mixture. Bake at 350 degrees for 1 hour.

Serves 6

IRONS IN THE FIRE • MEATS

At a Wednesday Pro-Am tournament, I noticed that one of my playing partners had a shiny new set of irons, new woods and a new bag. I remarked about the great equipment with my partner and asked him how long he had been playing. Excitedly the man explained that he had just retired and that the clubs and the spot in the tournament were retirement gifts from his co-workers. The tournament was his first time ever to play golf!

CHEDDAR MEAT LOAVES

Doug Tewell

1 egg
3/4 cup milk
1 cup shredded Cheddar cheese
1/2 cup quick-cooking oats
1/2 cup chopped onion
1 teaspoon salt
1 pound lean ground beef
2/3 cup ketchup
1/2 cup packed brown sugar
1 1/2 teaspoons prepared mustard

Beat the egg with the milk in a mixing bowl. Stir in the cheese, oats, onion and salt. Add the ground beef and mix well. Shape into 8 small loaves and place in a greased 9×13-inch baking dish.

Combine the ketchup, brown sugar and mustard in a small bowl and mix well. Spread over the meat loaves. Insert a meat thermometer into the thickest portion of 1 loaf. Bake at 350 degrees for 45 minutes or until the meat thermometer registers 160 degrees.

Serves 8

MEATBALLS

Ed Dougherty

*For a quick meal, heat the meatballs with a jar of spaghetti sauce and
serve on bread or rolls as meatball sandwiches.*

1^{1}/$_{2}$ pounds ground beef
2 cups fresh French or Italian bread crumbs
1 cup grated Parmesan cheese
^{1}/$_{2}$ cup chopped fresh parsley
1 teaspoon salt
^{1}/$_{2}$ teaspoon pepper
2 eggs
^{1}/$_{4}$ cup water
4 to 5 tablespoons vegetable oil
spaghetti sauce
hot cooked pasta

Combine the ground beef with the bread crumbs, Parmesan cheese, parsley,
salt and pepper in a bowl. Beat the eggs with the water in a small bowl. Add to
the ground beef mixture and mix well. Shape into 20 to 25 meatballs.

Heat the vegetable oil in a skillet and add the meatballs. Cook until brown,
turning to brown evenly; drain.

Add the meatballs to the spaghetti sauce in a saucepan and simmer for
30 minutes. Serve over pasta.

You may substitute ground pork and/or veal for part of the ground beef
if desired.

Serves 6

IRONS IN THE FIRE • MEATS

Golf pros who play on the Tour for many years sometimes have fans that become close friends. Just such an elderly couple became good friends of Hugh and his wife on the regular Tour in Europe. Because it was a long flight to South Africa, they decided to come for a six-week visit. The Baiocchis enjoyed them, but there was a significant difference in their ages, and after a while it became a bit of a challenge for them. They did not realize that their seven-year-old son heard them discussing the problems of the protracted visit. One day as they were driving to a golf course, their son asked the visitor, "Are you returning home on Tuesday?" Their guest replied, "No, we are leaving on Saturday. Why? Do you wish to get rid of us?" To which Justin answered, "No, but my dad does."

POTATO BURGER PIE

Hugh Baiocchi

1 pound ground beef
1 pound potatoes, peeled, grated
1 large onion, grated
1 (8-ounce) can tomatoes
1 tablespoon chopped parsley
salt and pepper to taste

Combine the ground beef, potatoes, onion and undrained tomatoes in a bowl. Add the parsley, salt and pepper and mix well. Spoon into a baking dish. Bake, covered, at 325 degrees for 1 hour. Bake, uncovered, for 30 minutes longer.

Serves 4

When golf pros go on vacation, we go home! After spending as many as 35 weeks a year traveling, the last thing most of us want to do is pack a suitcase and board another airplane. We spend our vacations at home with family and friends. Occasionally, the lure of a "real" vacation wins us over and off we go, but for the most part, we just enjoy being home.

CRUSTLESS HAM QUICHE

Billy Casper

1 cup (2 sticks) butter

10 eggs, beaten

1 pound ham, chopped

1/2 cup flour

1 teaspoon baking powder

2 cups cottage cheese

1 pound cheese, shredded

2 (4-ounce) cans chopped green chiles

1 teaspoon salt or garlic salt

Melt the butter in a skillet. Add the eggs and cook until soft-set, stirring constantly. Combine the eggs, ham, flour, baking powder, cottage cheese, Cheddar cheese, green chiles and salt in a bowl and mix well.

Spoon into a 9×13-inch baking dish. Bake at 350 degrees for 35 minutes or until a knife inserted in the center comes out clean. Serve with salsa and guacamole.

Serves 8

One night when I was alone in our house in Palm Springs, I decided to heat a tray of egg rolls for a small dinner. When I put the rolls in the oven, I noticed a small lever on the oven door, so I slid it across. One hour later I had a self-cleaned oven and a dozen black egg rolls.

SAVORY OVEN-ROASTED BISON MEATBALLS

Dave Stockton

To serve bison meatballs as an appetizer, prepare a dipping sauce of 2/3 cup low-fat mayonnaise, 1/3 cup Dijon mustard and 1 tablespoon chopped green onion.

1 pound lean ground bison	1 teaspoon Italian seasoning
1/2 cup finely chopped mushrooms	1 teaspoon salt
1/3 cup finely chopped red onion	1 teaspoon pepper
2 garlic cloves, minced	marinara sauce or Swedish meatball sauce
1 egg, beaten	hot cooked wide egg noodles

Combine the first 8 ingredients in a medium bowl and mix well. Shape into twenty-four 1-inch meatballs. Arrange the meatballs on a baking sheet sprayed with nonstick cooking spray. Roast at 400 degrees for 10 minutes. Add the meatballs to desired sauce in a saucepan and cook until heated through. Serve over noodles.

Serves 4

Dave Stockton with sons Dave Jr. and Ronnie

Bison Lasagna

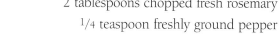

Dave Stockton

8 ounces ground bison

1 onion, chopped

4 garlic cloves, minced

2 large tomatoes, peeled, seeded, chopped

1/4 cup beef broth or beef stock

2 tablespoons chopped fresh oregano

2 tablespoons chopped fresh rosemary

1/4 teaspoon freshly ground pepper

2 cups ricotta cheese

2 teaspoons grated Parmesan cheese

1 cup chopped fresh basil

1/2 cup chopped oil-pack sun-dried tomatoes

4 garlic cloves

9 uncooked lasagna noodles

6 quarts boiling water

1 1/2 cups shredded mozzarella cheese

Spray a large nonstick skillet with nonstick cooking spray and heat over medium heat. Add the ground bison, onion and 4 minced garlic cloves and cook for 5 minutes, stirring until the ground bison is brown and crumbly; drain.

Add the chopped tomatoes, beef broth, oregano, rosemary and pepper. Bring to a boil and reduce the heat to low. Simmer for 10 minutes or until thickened. Remove from the heat.

Combine the ricotta cheese, Parmesan cheese, basil, sun-dried tomatoes and 4 garlic cloves in a food processor container. Process until smooth.

Cook the lasagna noodles in the water in a large saucepan for 10 minutes or until al dente; drain. Arrange 3 of the noodles in a 9×13-inch baking dish sprayed with nonstick cooking spray. Layer with half the ricotta cheese mixture, 1/3 of the meat sauce and 1/3 of the mozzarella cheese. Repeat the layers. Top with the remaining noodles, remaining meat sauce and remaining mozzarella cheese.

Bake at 350 degrees for 35 to 60 minutes or until bubbly and golden brown on the top. Let stand for 10 minutes before serving.

Serves 6

Bison meat has a sweeter and richer flavor than beef. The value of bison is not what it costs, but what you get in return. Nutritionally, bison has more protein and nutrients with fewer calories and less fat and cholesterol than beef, chicken or pork. A smaller serving of the dense meat tends to be more satisfying.

Our bison range or graze on the lush meadow grasses of the Sierra Nevada Mountains on our Cooks Creek Ranch in northern California. We do not supplement with growth hormones or chemicals. They are a pure breed without cross-breeding or genetic alteration.

Dave and Cathy Stockton with Soo Ling

When my son/caddy Brian and I arrived in Narita, Japan, we brought along a week's dirty laundry from the previous week of playing in California. No problem—we just took it to the front desk and dropped it off. We picked it up the next morning along with a whopping bill for $312. It was the start of a week that just got worse. There was a small earthquake that morning. When play resumed all seemed to go well until the last day, when it snowed so heavily the tournament was called after nine holes. On the way to the airport our busload of golfers had to detour around airport protesters to a safer place, where armed guards and policemen escorted us to our plane.

HONEY GINGER PORK TENDERLOIN

DeWitt Weaver

1/4 cup honey

1/4 cup soy sauce

1 tablespoon ketchup

2 tablespoons brown sugar

1 tablespoon minced garlic

1 tablespoon minced fresh gingerroot

1/4 teaspoon ground cinnamon

1/4 teaspoon ground red pepper

2 (12-ounce) pork tenderloins

Combine the honey, soy sauce, ketchup, brown sugar, garlic, gingerroot, cinnamon and red pepper in a bowl and mix well. Pour over the tenderloins in a 7×11-inch dish. Marinate in the refrigerator for 8 hours, turning occasionally.

Drain the tenderloins, reserving the marinade. Pour the marinade into a saucepan and bring to a boil.

Insert a meat thermometer into the thickest portion of 1 tenderloin and place the tenderloins on a grill over coals heated medium hot, 350 to 400 degrees. Grill, covered, to 160 degrees on the meat thermometer, turning and basting frequently with the marinade.

Cut into thin slices and arrange on a serving platter. Garnish with fresh parsley.

Serves 6

IRONS IN THE FIRE • MEATS

Chi Chi once commented about Pro-Am players' approach to golf: "These people are on the first tee, look down the middle, aim left, hit right, holler fore, score seven and write down five."

HAWAIIAN ROAST PORK

Chi Chi Rodriguez

1 (5-pound) pork roast	12 large ti leaves
liquid smoke	12 sweet potatoes
Hawaiian salt	12 bananas

Cut slits in the pork roast and brush on all sides with liquid smoke. Sprinkle with Hawaiian salt to taste. Wrap the roast with ti leaves and tie with string. Wrap in foil.

Place on a rack in a roasting pan. Roast at 350 degrees for 3½ hours. Add sweet potatoes to the roasting pan. Roast for 1 hour. Add bananas to the roasting pan. Roast for 30 minutes longer.

Serves 12

We took both of our children to my first SENIOR TOUR event, being held in Seattle. I had met a wonderful man at the Pro-Am Tournament who owned a salmon canning company. He invited our family and a long-time family friend, Harry Swimmer, to go salmon fishing with him on Puget Sound. It was very cold and windy, but we all went along. Shortly after leaving the dock, smoke began billowing from the engine compartment. Our captain told us that he was going to drive us over to a nearby dock and that we needed to get off the boat immediately upon arriving there. All our friend Harry heard, however, was "get off the boat immediately." With that, he dove into the freezing cold water. We all made it to the dock safely, but 12 years later, we still laugh about "Swimmer the swimmer" at our first SENIOR TOUR event.

PORK CHOP CASSEROLE

Larry Ziegler

4 boneless pork chops

2 tablespoons vegetable oil

4 cups thinly sliced potatoes

1 (10-ounce) can cream of mushroom or cream of chicken soup

$^1/_2$ cup sour cream

$^1/_4$ cup water

$^1/_2$ cup shredded Cheddar cheese

Brown the pork chops on both sides in the vegetable oil in a skillet. Remove to a 2-quart baking dish. Arrange the potato slices over the pork chops. Combine the soup, sour cream and water in a bowl and mix well. Spread over the potatoes.

Bake, covered, at 375 degrees for 1$^1/_2$ hours or until the pork chops are tender. Sprinkle with the cheese. Bake until the cheese melts.

Serves 4

IRONS IN THE FIRE • MEATS

FILETTO DI MAIALE ARROSTO

Gary Player

PORK	**APPLE SAUCE**
2 garlic cloves, crushed	6 green apples, peeled, cored, sliced
salt and pepper to taste	1 liter red wine
1 pork loin, trimmed, tied	3 tablespoons balsamic vinegar
500 milliliters dry white wine	2 teaspoons honey
300 grams unsalted butter	

For the pork, rub the garlic, salt and pepper over the pork loin and place it in a roasting pan. Pour the wine over the pork and spread with the butter. Roast, covered with foil, at 200 degrees centigrade (390 degrees Fahrenheit) for 2 hours.

For the sauce, combine the apples with the wine, vinegar and honey in a saucepan. Simmer until the apples are tender. Process the mixture in a food processor until smooth. Return the apple sauce to the saucepan and cook until reduced by half.

To serve, slice the pork and arrange on serving plates. Spoon the apple sauce over the slices. Garnish with a fan of additional sliced green apples. Serve with creamed spinach and a butternut and potato casserole.

Refer to the Metric Conversion Chart on page 215 for measurement equivalents.

Serves 12

Some Senior moments on Tour come at the expense of our Pro-Am partners. Recently in Dearborn, an amateur partner and his group started on the back nine. When they got to number 17, a par five bordered by water on the left side, he chipped the ball from the right side just by the hole. He walked up to the ball, marked it and took a few steps back. Before his team could warn him, he backed right off the green into the lake and went completely under. He climbed back out onto the green where everyone was laughing so hard they were almost crying. He was so embarrassed about the incident that he skipped hole 18 and went to the pro shop where he purchased a new outfit—all but the jockey shorts, which the pro shop didn't sell. He looked great, but was still wet around the middle since he didn't like the idea of playing "au naturel."

CHORIZO FRITTATA

Jim Ahern

1/2 cup chopped onion

1/2 cup chopped red bell pepper

2 tablespoons butter

2 chorizo links, sliced

4 eggs, beaten

salt and pepper to taste

1/2 cup shredded Swiss, Monterey Jack, and/or mozzarella cheese

Sauté the onion and bell pepper in the butter in an ovenproof skillet over medium heat until golden brown. Add the chorizo and sauté for several minutes longer. Reduce the heat.

Add the eggs. Sprinkle with salt, pepper and cheese. Cook until the eggs are set on the bottom. Broil for 3 minutes or until the cheese melts and the eggs are set on the top. Cut into wedges to serve.

Serves 6

IRONS IN THE FIRE • MEATS

At the St. Jude Classic in Memphis, Tennessee, Federal Express is a major sponsor. As a courtesy to the players, FedEx ships packages anywhere free of charge. The players ship just about anything, but Ed topped them all. One of his hobbies is 1958 Chevy Impalas, and he owns a couple that he keeps in Philadelphia. While at the tournament, Ed got a deal on a '58 Chevy that he could use for parts, so he had a mechanic take it apart, and he asked FedEx if they could ship it home for him. Without missing a beat, the FedEx representative, who has dealt with the players for years, asked if he would like that delivered overnight. So Ed had a car packed into 16 boxes and sent home overnight.

ITALIAN PASTA SAUCE

Ed Dougherty

Add the meatballs on page 68 to this sauce for a heartier dish. The recipe makes a lot of sauce, but it can be frozen.

1 cup chopped onion	1/2 cup chopped fresh Italian parsley
4 or 5 garlic cloves, chopped	1/4 cup chopped fresh basil
1/4 cup olive oil	1 (12-ounce) can tomato paste
1 (28-ounce) can crushed tomatoes	1/2 cup grated Parmesan or Romano cheese
1 (28-ounce) can plum tomatoes	1 tablespoon sugar
1 (28-ounce) can puréed tomatoes	salt and black pepper to taste
1 cup water	1/2 teaspoon cayenne pepper (optional)
8 ounces Italian sausage	

Sauté the onion and garlic in the heated olive oil in an 8- to 10-quart stockpot until tender. Add the crushed tomatoes, plum tomatoes, puréed tomatoes and water and mix well. Bring to a low boil.

Brown the sausage in a skillet, stirring until crumbly; drain. Add to the tomato mixture with the parsley and basil. Reduce the heat and simmer for 30 minutes.

Stir in the tomato paste and cheese. Simmer for 1 hour, stirring occasionally. Add the sugar, salt, black pepper and cayenne pepper. Serve over pasta.

You may use any combination of the canned tomatoes that you prefer.

Serves 12

I was playing in the Bing Crosby Tournament in Pebble Beach, California, when Bing came over to talk to me. My wife in the gallery said to our daughter, "See that man talking to your daddy? That's Bing Crosby." Our daughter replied, "That's Bing Crosby? Why did he name himself after a golf tournament?"

LASAGNA

George Archer

1 (16-ounce) package lasagna noodles

2 cups ricotta cheese

$1/2$ cup grated Parmesan cheese

2 eggs, beaten

1 tablespoon parsley flakes

$1^1/2$ pounds Italian sausage, casings removed

1 small onion, chopped

2 tablespoons chopped garlic

2 tablespoons olive oil

2 teaspoons basil

1 (22-ounce) can stewed tomatoes

2 (6-ounce) cans tomato paste

sliced Monterey Jack, sharp Cheddar and mozzarella cheese

Cook the noodles using the package directions; drain and separate the noodles. Mix the ricotta cheese, Parmesan cheese, eggs and parsley flakes in a bowl.

Brown the sausage in a skillet, stirring until crumbly; drain. Remove to a bowl. Sauté the onion and garlic in the olive oil in the skillet until translucent. Add to the sausage. Stir in the basil, undrained tomatoes and tomato paste.

Reserve $1/3$ of the sausage mixture. Layer the noodles, remaining sausage mixture, sliced cheese and ricotta mixture $1/2$ at a time in a 9×13-inch baking dish. Top with the reserved sausage mixture.

Bake at 375 degrees for 40 minutes. Let stand for 10 minutes before serving.

Serves 12

SAUSAGE CASSEROLE
....
Miller Barber

*Serve this with grits for breakfast, or substitute crumbled bleu cheese for the
Cheddar cheese and add a salad to serve it for dinner.*

1 pound hot bulk sausage
1 onion, chopped
1/2 cup (or more) salsa
2 cups shredded Cheddar cheese
1 (8-ounce) package corn muffin mix
1 egg
1/3 cup milk

Brown the sausage with the onion in an 8- or 9-inch cast-iron skillet over
medium heat, stirring until the sausage is crumbly. Drain the skillet and arrange
the sausage evenly over the bottom of the skillet. Layer the salsa and cheese over
the sausage.

Combine the corn muffin mix with the egg and milk in a bowl and mix just
until moistened. Pour over the layers in the skillet.

Bake at 400 degrees for 20 minutes or until golden brown. Invert onto a
serving platter and serve immediately.

Serves 6 to 8

I am one of a number of players who sometimes has a family member such as a child, a grandchild, a son-in-law or a daughter-in-law as a caddy. Some of the others who do include: Jim Albus, George Archer, Butch Baird, Miller Barber, Don Bies, John Bland, Bob Charles, Jim Colbert, Charles Coody, Jim Dent, Allen Doyle, Bob Eastwood, Vincente Fernandez, Raymond Floyd, Al Geiberger, Gibby Gilbert, Bob Gilder, David Graham, Hubert Green, Mark Hayes, Mike Hill, Joe Inman, Jr., Hale Irwin, Tom Kite, David Lundstrom, Graham Marsh, Jerry McGee, Orville Moody, Larry Nelson, Bobby Nichols, Jack Nicklaus, Andy North, Christy O'Connor, Jr., Arnold Palmer, Gary Player, Dana Quigley, JC Snead, Dave Stockton, Bruce Summerhays, Doug Tewell, Lee Trevino, DeWitt Weaver, Tom Weiskopf, Kermit Zarley and Larry Ziegler.

BUTTERFLIED LEG OF LAMB

Bob Murphy

1 (7- to 8-pound) leg of lamb, trimmed, boned, butterflied
1 (16-ounce) bottle Italian salad dressing
3 or 4 handfuls fresh mint leaves

Place the lamb open in a large dish and pour the salad dressing over the top. Sprinkle the mint over the lamb. Marinate, covered, in the refrigerator for 8 hours, turning and replacing the mint on the top every 4 hours, or for longer without turning. Drain, reserving the mint.

Grill the lamb over medium-high coals until nearly done to taste, turning frequently. Place the reserved mint on top of the lamb and grill until done to taste. Remove to a serving plate and slice diagonally. Serve with the mint, fresh corn, a tossed salad, French bread and a bottle of Chateau Montelena or Silver Oak Cabernet Sauvignon.

Serves 6

IRONS IN THE FIRE • MEATS

While playing at the Bing Crosby Tournament, I hit a wayward drive behind a tree at Cypress Point. As I approached the tree I could smell pipe smoke. As I walked up and looked at my ball, Bing Crosby, pipe in mouth, stuck his head around the tree and said, "Not all the trees at Cypress Point are beautiful, are they?"

ROAST LEG OF LAMB WITH MINT SAUCE

Graham Marsh

1 leg of lamb
garlic cloves, cut into slivers
salt to taste
freshly ground pepper to taste
2 tablespoons finely chopped fresh mint leaves
2 teaspoons sugar
1 tablespoon boiling water
2 tablespoons white vinegar

Cut slits in the leg of lamb and insert the slivers of garlic into the slits; rub with salt and pepper. Place on a rack in a roasting pan. Roast at 350 degrees for 30 minutes per pound for medium.

Sprinkle the mint with the sugar in a bowl and pour the boiling water over the top. Stir until the sugar dissolves. Cool to room temperature and stir in the vinegar.

Pour the mint mixture over the lamb. Let stand in a warm place for 15 minutes before slicing to serve.

Serves 8

MEATS • IRONS IN THE FIRE

PICNIC LAMB SHANKS

Gary Player

4 to 6 whole lamb shanks (about 3 to 4 pounds), trimmed
1/2 teaspoon rosemary
1/2 teaspoon thyme, crumbled
1/8 teaspoon ground cloves
1/2 teaspoon salt
1/4 teaspoon pepper
1 garlic clove, crushed or minced
1 bay leaf
3 tablespoons lemon juice
1/3 cup red wine or water

Place the lamb shanks in a heavy baking dish or pan. Sprinkle with the rosemary, thyme, cloves, salt and pepper. Add the garlic, bay leaf, lemon juice and wine. Roast, covered, at 425 degrees for 1 1/2 hours or until tender, turning 2 or 3 times. Cool in the cooking liquid; discard the bay leaf.

Drain the lamb, reserving the cooking liquid. Grill 3 inches from medium-hot coals for 15 to 20 minutes or until rich brown and heated through, basting occasionally with the reserved liquid.

Wrap the bony ends with foil to serve for eating out of hand.

Serves 4 to 6

LANCASHIRE HOT POT

John Morgan

1^1/2 pounds best-end neck of lamb
2 lamb kidneys, skinned, cored
2 carrots, peeled, sliced
1 small turnip, peeled, sliced
8 ounces onions, chopped
1 leek, chopped
salt and pepper to taste
1 pound potatoes, peeled, sliced
1 to 1^1/2 cups water or stock
2 tablespoons butter

Cut the lamb neck and kidneys into bite-size pieces. Layer the lamb, kidneys, carrots, turnip, onions and leek in a baking dish. Season with salt and pepper. Arrange the potato slices in an overlapping layer over the top. Add water to ^{1}/3 of the depth of the dish. Dot with butter.

Bake, covered, at 350 degrees for 1^1/2 hours. Increase the oven temperature to 400 degrees and bake, uncovered, for 30 minutes longer or until the potatoes are golden brown. Garnish with parsley.

You may broil to brown the top if preferred.

Serves 4

Ah, the old popcorn popper. Bet you thought it was only for popping corn. While popcorn is a favorite snack, in early days of Tour traveling it was also used for heating soup, baby food, macaroni and cheese, spaghetti, boiled eggs and much more.

NEW ZEALAND RACKS OF LAMB

Bob Charles

4 small prime racks of lamb
lemon juice to taste
salt and pepper to taste
grainy mustard to taste
4 sprigs of fresh rosemary

Sprinkle the lamb with lemon juice. Season with salt and pepper and spread with mustard. Place on a rack in a roasting pan and place a sprig of rosemary on each rack.

Roast at 500 degrees for 10 minutes. Let stand for 5 minutes before serving.

Serves 4

There are some words and phrases that we have to teach each other as we travel on the Tour. Americans need to learn that a boot is the trunk of a car and the bonnet is the hood; a handbag is a purse, but a purse is a wallet; a robot is a traffic light; a biscuit is a cracker; a lift is an elevator; and biltong is beef jerky.

SCALOPPINI ALLA CASALINGA

Gary Player

4 boneless veal cutlets
flour
olive oil
4 slices provolone cheese
napoli sauce or marinara sauce

Coat the veal cutlets with flour. Sauté in heated olive oil in an oven-proof skillet until light brown on both sides and done to taste.

Place a slice of cheese on each cutlet and top with the napoli sauce. Broil just until the cheese melts and the sauce is bubbly. Serve immediately.

Serves 4

IRONS IN THE FIRE • MEATS

I was playing in a tournament at the old Sawgrass Golf Course. I was hitting my second shot from about 60 yards on the fourth green, which is on two levels, when a big gust of wind came up. I saw my Panama hat roll down the fairway on its brim and up onto the green. The hat rolled to the back of the second level where the pin was and struck my ball, thus incurring a two-stroke penalty. I went on to three-putt the hole.

VENISON

J. C. Snead

venison
salt water
garlic cloves, crushed
1/2 cup (1 stick) butter, melted

Slice the venison 1 inch thick and combine with a mild solution of salt water in a bowl. Soak while preparing the grill. Combine the garlic and melted butter in a small bowl.

Drain the venison and place on a grill over hot coals. Grill for 2 minutes. Turn the venison and brush with the garlic butter. Grill just until done to taste; do not overcook, as venison will become tough. Serve with mashed potatoes, creamed peas, sliced tomatoes and buttermilk biscuits.

To prevent a gamey taste of venison, always skin it as soon as possible; never leave it overnight.

Makes a variable amount

BIRDIES

AND

BUNKERS

POULTRY • SEAFOOD

I was having a good time playing in the Tuesday shootout in Boone County and found myself tied with Hale Irwin going into the last hole. If I made my putt, I would win it all, so I decided that I would pick someone out of the crowd to putt my ball. I chose a woman who was seated next to the green. It turned out that she had never played golf. I lined her up and she made the putt! We have kept in contact with her ever since.

CREAMED CHICKEN PAPRIKASH

Tom Wargo

1/2 cup finely chopped onion

3 tablespoons shortening

1 (3- to 4-pound) chicken, cut up

2 cups water

1 tablespoon paprika

2 tablespoons salt

1 tablespoon flour

1 cup sour cream

Sauté the onion in the shortening in a saucepan until translucent. Add the chicken and cook, covered, over low heat until the chicken begins to stick to the saucepan.

Add the water, paprika and salt. Cook, covered, for 1 hour. Blend the flour and sour cream in a small bowl. Add to the saucepan and cook for 5 minutes, stirring frequently. Serve with dumplings.

Serves 4 to 6

BIRDIES AND BUNKERS • POULTRY • SEAFOOD

We do more than play golf when we are on Tour. During the Michigan tournament one year, we went fishing on Lake Michigan with the Stocktons. The water was really rough and my wife Sandi and I got seasick. I did her one better by fainting straight backwards and scaring everyone to death. The captain immediately aborted the trip and took us back to shore, where my legs were much happier. That winter we vacationed with Cathy and Dave in Cabo, and when we arrived I asked when we were fishing with the boys on the next day. Dave replied, "Lotz, you're staying behind to golf with the girls. I'm not coming in early again!" It took two years before I got back out deep-sea fishing with the boys in Cabo, but I showed them: I caught the most fish!

CALIFORNIA CHICKEN

Dick Lotz

4 chicken breasts
1 garlic clove, crushed
1 tablespoon olive oil
roasted red peppers (optional)
4 slices mozzarella cheese
tortilla chips
1 or 2 avocados, mashed
sour cream

Cook the chicken with the garlic in the olive oil in a skillet over low heat, turning frequently. Top each with roasted red peppers and a slice of cheese and simmer until the cheese melts.

Crush tortilla chips and place on serving plates. Place 1 piece of chicken on each plate and top with avocado and sour cream. Serve with hot salsa.

Serves 4

Bob's wife Shari noticed that Bob was limping down the fairway at the Boone Valley Senior Classic. He stopped and took off his shoe, emptied it, put it back on and continued limping. He then went to his cart, removed both his shoe and sock and emptied them. He picked something up off the ground and looked at her. He replaced his shoe, walked over the rope line and said, "Did you lose something?" He then handed her one of her fake fingernails, which had been lost, probably while doing the laundry.

FAVORITE CHICKEN CASSEROLE

Bob Duval

2 large white onions, thinly sliced
6 to 8 boneless skinless chicken breasts
6 to 8 slices Swiss cheese
2 (10-ounce) cans cream of chicken soup
1/2 cup white wine
1 envelope chicken gravy mix
white Worcestershire sauce to taste
dried bread crumb stuffing mix
1/2 cup (1 stick) butter, melted

Layer the onion slices and chicken in a 9×13-inch baking dish sprayed with nonstick cooking spray. Place 1 slice of cheese on each piece of chicken. Combine the chicken soup, wine, gravy mix and Worcestershire sauce in a bowl and mix well. Spoon over the chicken.

Sprinkle with the stuffing mix and drizzle with the butter. Bake at 350 degrees for 40 to 45 minutes or until the top is golden brown and the chicken is cooked through. Serve with a salad and rolls.

Serves 4 to 6

BIRDIES AND BUNKERS • POULTRY • SEAFOOD

Back in our days on the European Tour, John Bland and I were paired together at the German Open. We were playing number 17, a long par five, and I had hit my third shot about 25 feet from the hole. I used an Italian coin as my ball marker and walked behind the hole to check my line. When I walked back, however, I noticed that my marker was now about ten feet from the hole. I absolutely froze and tried to imagine how I had managed to move the marker. Could I have kicked it or hit it with my putter? The next thought that crossed my mind was: How will I get the marker back to its correct spot? I turned to Bland and said, "I have a problem here," and his reply was, "How long has it been going on?" referring to how long I had been juggling on the green. I began to bluster in an attempt to explain, when he told me that he had, in fact, dropped a coin in my line, causing all the chaos.

CHICKEN A LA KING

Hugh Baiocchi

2 pounds boneless skinless chicken tenders or breasts
1 medium onion, chopped
1 tablespoon instant chicken bouillon granules
1 (5-ounce) can reduced-fat evaporated milk
Tabasco sauce to taste
salt and pepper to taste
2 tablespoons cornstarch

Cut the chicken into bite-size pieces. Combine with the onion, chicken bouillon and enough water to cover in a saucepan. Simmer, covered, until the chicken is tender. Drain, reserving the cooking liquid.

Combine the evaporated milk with enough of the reserved liquid to make the desired amount of gravy in a saucepan. Season with Tabasco sauce, salt and pepper. Blend the cornstarch with enough cold water to make a paste in a cup. Add to the saucepan.

Cook until thickened, stirring constantly. Add the chicken and cook until heated through. Serve over rice with a salad.

Serves 6

CHICKEN AND RICE CASSEROLE WITH ASPARAGUS

Hubert Green

4 to 6 boneless skinless chicken breasts

$1/4$ cup ($1/2$ stick) butter

5 tablespoons sifted flour

1 teaspoon salt

$2^1/2$ cups milk

$1^1/4$ cups uncooked instant rice

onion flakes to taste

1 (16-ounce) can asparagus spears, drained

2 cups shredded sharp Cheddar cheese

pepper to taste

toasted sliced almonds

Cook the chicken in water to cover in a saucepan until cooked through; drain, reserving $1^1/2$ cups chicken broth. Cut the chicken into bite-size pieces.

Melt the butter in a heavy saucepan. Stir in the flour and salt and cook until bubbly. Add the milk and cook until thickened and smooth, stirring constantly.

Sprinkle the rice and onion flakes in a 1- to 2-quart baking dish sprayed with nonstick cooking spray. Add 1 cup of the reserved chicken broth. Arrange the asparagus over the rice.

Sprinkle the cheese and pepper over the asparagus and top with the chicken. Pour the remaining $1/2$ cup reserved chicken broth over the chicken.

Spread the white sauce over the top and sprinkle with the almonds. Bake at 350 degrees for 20 to 30 minutes or until bubbly.

You may freeze this casserole, thaw it and reheat to serve.

Serves 6

Gene Littler's first professional trip was to Las Vegas for the Tournament of Champions. He pulled up to the front of the Desert Inn with his new car and trailer. The tournament officials were horrified. This was a first-class event and all the players were to be housed in the plush hotel and not at some trailer park on the outskirts of town as sometimes happened. Gene looked around and said, "Guess I have to get used to this!"

CHICKEN JUBILEE

Gene Littler

1/2 cup flour
1/2 teaspoon paprika
1/4 teaspoon garlic salt
1 1/2 teaspoons salt
6 to 8 boneless skinless chicken breasts
1/4 cup vegetable oil or shortening
1 cup chicken broth or white wine
2 cups pitted Bing cherries in heavy syrup
1/2 cup brandy

Combine the flour, paprika, garlic salt and salt in a bag. Add the chicken and shake to coat well. Cook in the vegetable oil in a skillet over low heat until golden brown on both sides. Remove to a baking pan and pour the chicken broth into the pan.

Bake, covered, at 375 degrees for 15 to 20 minutes. Add the cherries and bake, uncovered, for 10 to 15 minutes longer or until the chicken is tender.

Place the baking pan on the stove top and add the brandy. Cook just until the brandy is heated; do not boil. Ignite the brandy and allow the flames to die down. Serve with the cherries and sauce.

Serves 6 to 8

FETTUCCINI WITH CHICKEN AND SPINACH

Jay Sigel

1 onion, chopped
2 garlic cloves, minced
2 tablespoons chopped fresh basil
1/2 teaspoon red pepper flakes
1/2 cup (1 stick) butter
1 pound boneless skinless chicken breasts, cut into strips
2 (10-ounce) packages frozen chopped spinach, thawed
salt and pepper to taste
12 ounces fettuccini, cooked, drained
2 cups grated fresh Parmesan cheese
1 1/2 tablespoons orange juice

Sauté the onion and garlic with the basil and red pepper flakes in the melted butter in a large skillet over medium heat for 7 minutes or until the onion is tender. Add the chicken and sauté for 10 minutes, stirring frequently.

Press the spinach to remove the excess moisture. Add to the skillet and season with salt and pepper. Cook until heated through.

Combine the hot pasta, chicken mixture and cheese in a serving bowl and toss to mix well. Drizzle with the orange juice.

Serves 4

HOT CHICKEN SALAD CASSEROLE

Jack Nicklaus

3 cups chopped cooked chicken

1 cup slivered almonds

1 (8-ounce) can sliced water
chestnuts, drained

1 (4-ounce) can sliced pimentos, drained

2 cups chopped celery

1 (10-ounce) can cream of chicken soup

1 cup shredded Cheddar cheese

1 1/2 cups mayonnaise

1 tablespoon lemon juice

1 teaspoon salt

1/2 teaspoon pepper

1 (3-ounce) can French-fried onions

Combine the chicken, almonds, water chestnuts, pimentos, celery, soup, cheese, mayonnaise, lemon juice, salt and pepper in a large bowl and mix well. Spoon into a 9×13-inch baking dish.

Bake at 325 degrees for 35 minutes. Sprinkle with the onions and bake for 10 minutes longer. Let stand for 10 minutes. Cut into squares to serve.

Serves 8 to 12

Jack Nicklaus with sons Steve and Jackie

King Ranch Casserole

Charles Coody and Tom Kite

1 ($2^{1}/_{2}$- to 3-pound) chicken

1 bay leaf

salt to taste

1 (10-ounce) can cream of mushroom soup

1 (10-ounce) can cream of chicken soup

$^{1}/_{2}$ to 1 (10-ounce) can tomatoes with green chiles

12 corn tortillas

1 large onion, chopped

1 cup chopped celery

1 to 2 cups shredded Cheddar cheese

Combine the chicken with water to cover in a large saucepan. Add the bay leaf and salt to taste. Bring to a boil and reduce the heat. Simmer for 45 to 60 minutes or until the chicken is tender. Drain, reserving 1 cup of the chicken broth, discarding the bay leaf. Cut the chicken into bite-size pieces, discarding the skin and bones.

Combine the mushroom soup, chicken soup, undrained tomatoes with green chiles and reserved chicken broth in a bowl and mix well.

Arrange $^{1}/_{3}$ of the tortillas in a 9×13-inch baking dish. Layer $^{1}/_{3}$ of the chicken, half the onion, half the celery, $^{1}/_{3}$ of the soup mixture and $^{1}/_{3}$ of the cheese in the prepared dish.

Repeat the layers and top with the remaining tortillas, chicken, soup mixture and cheese. Bake at 350 degrees for 40 to 50 minutes or until bubbly.

Serves 8 to 10

SUMPTUOUS CHICKEN

....

Bruce Fleisher

3/4 cup flour

1 1/2 teaspoons paprika

2 teaspoons salt

1/2 teaspoon pepper

6 pounds chicken pieces or breasts

1/4 cup (1/2 stick) butter

1/4 cup shortening

1 1/4 cups water

1 (10-ounce) can beef consommé

2 tablespoons ketchup

1 cup sour cream

1 (13-ounce) can cling peach halves, drained

1 cup grated Parmesan cheese

Combine the flour, paprika, salt and pepper in a bag. Add the chicken and shake to coat well. Shake off the excess flour mixture from the chicken and reserve the remaining flour mixture. Brown the chicken on both sides in the butter and shortening in a large skillet. Remove the chicken to paper towels to drain. Place in a 9×13-inch baking dish.

Stir the reserved flour mixture into the drippings remaining in the skillet. Cook until bubbly. Add the water, consommé and ketchup gradually. Cook until thickened, stirring constantly. Remove from the heat and stir in the sour cream. Spoon over the chicken.

Bake, covered with foil, at 375 degrees for 40 minutes. Arrange the peach halves cut side up on the chicken and sprinkle evenly with the cheese. Bake, uncovered, for 10 minutes longer. Serve with rice and a vegetable.

Serves 6 to 8

I just don't know how we managed the travel on the Tour in the 60s and 70s. We traveled with sterilizers, cloth diapers, tricycles, toys, electric skillets, portable grills, clothes and golf clubs in our cars and station wagons. Everyone traveled by car, including the leading money winners. We all pulled together and helped each other, even though we were competing. We usually all stayed in the same motels and tried to find places with kitchenettes so that we could "eat in." There were few fast-food places, and meals were not provided by the tournaments. We babysat for each other, car pooled and enjoyed lots of cookouts together in those days.

CHICKEN OSSO BUCO

Johnny Pott

1 cup flour	3/4 cup chopped celery
1 teaspoon salt	2 garlic cloves, minced
1 teaspoon pepper	1 (8-ounce) can tomato sauce
12 chicken thighs	1 cup dry white wine
1/4 cup (1/2 stick) butter	2 teaspoons basil
1 cup chopped onion	2 teaspoons thyme
1 cup sliced carrots	

Combine the flour, salt and pepper in a bag. Add the chicken and shake to coat well. Brown the chicken on both sides in the heated butter in a large skillet. Remove to a plate.

Add the onion to the drippings in the skillet and sauté until tender. Add the carrots, celery, garlic, tomato sauce, wine, basil and thyme and mix well.

Return the chicken to the skillet. Simmer, covered, for 1 hour. Serve the chicken and sauce over rice.

Serves 6

Golfers feel fortunate to be able to fly around the world and play in different countries. One golfer tells of being asked to choose an entrée on a flight to New Zealand. He and his wife chose the fish, but their daughters thought sweetbreads sounded much better. They licked their plates clean thinking that they had pulled a fast one on Mom and Dad by having a sweet for their meal. When they learned what sweetbreads are two days later, they didn't find it as funny and, 20 years later, haven't made that choice again.

MEXICAN CASSEROLE

Raymond Floyd

3 cups chopped cooked chicken
1 cup nonfat sour cream
1 cup reduced-fat sour cream
2 (4-ounce) cans chopped green chiles, drained
$1^{1}/_{2}$ teaspoons chili powder
nonfat large tortillas
$1^{1}/_{2}$ (16-ounce) jars medium salsa
$1^{1}/_{2}$ cups shredded Cheddar and/or Monterey Jack cheese

Combine the chicken with the sour cream, green chiles and chili powder in a bowl and mix well.

Line the bottom of a baking dish with tortillas. Layer half the chicken mixture, salsa and cheese in the prepared dish. Add a second layer of tortillas and the remaining chicken mixture, salsa and cheese.

Bake at 350 degrees for 45 minutes or just until bubbly; do not overcook.

Serves 6 to 8

When my children were young, my wife had a rule that the doors would be locked at midnight. One night I decided to go out to play golf and cards. I got home late and discovered the door locked. I spent the night at a local Ramada Inn, and our children were never late for curfew.

MEXICAN CHICKEN AND BEAN CASSEROLE

Miller Barber

2 tablespoons chili powder
1 teaspoon garlic powder
1 teaspoon salt
1 teaspoon pepper
2 (16-ounce) cans black beans, drained
8 boneless skinless chicken breasts
olive oil
$^1/_2$ cup picante sauce
2 cups shredded Monterey Jack cheese

Mix the chili powder, garlic powder, salt and pepper together. Combine half the mixture with the black beans in a bowl and mix well.

Sprinkle the remaining seasoning mixture on the chicken. Sauté the chicken on both sides in a small amount of olive oil in a skillet. Remove the chicken to a baking dish and top each with 1 tablespoon picante sauce. Spread the beans over the chicken and sprinkle with the cheese.

Bake, covered with foil, at 350 degrees for 30 minutes. Bake, uncovered, until the cheese melts and the mixture is bubbly. Serve with a green salad and corn bread.

Serves 8

Cornish Game Hens with New Potatoes

Tom Jenkins

4 young Cornish game hens
2 tablespoons salt
1/4 cup fresh cracked pepper
16 small new potatoes
2 cups 2000 Wing Canyon Cabernet Sauvignon
1/2 cup extra-virgin olive oil
1 cup chopped fresh parsley
leaves of 1 bunch fresh rosemary
leaves of 1 bunch fresh thyme
2 bunches tender asparagus, steamed

Rinse the game hens inside and out and sprinkle the cavities generously with salt and pepper. Place in a roasting pan and add the new potatoes.

Combine the wine, olive oil, half the parsley, rosemary and thyme in a bowl and mix well. Pour into the cavities and over the game hens and new potatoes. Sprinkle the remaining parsley over the potatoes.

Bake at 375 degrees for 1 1/2 hours. Serve with the steamed asparagus and a 2000 Wing Canyon Cabernet Sauvignon.

Serves 4

TURKEY AND PENNE

....

Terry Dill

Use a cooked deli turkey breast to make this dish easy
enough to prepare "on Tour."

2 cups uncooked penne
2 cup chopped cooked turkey
1 zucchini, sliced
2 yellow squash, sliced
1 small green bell pepper, chopped
1 small red bell pepper, chopped
1/4 cup grated Parmesan cheese
1/2 to 3/4 cup ranch salad dressing

Cook the pasta using the package directions; rinse with cold water and drain.
Combine the pasta with the turkey, zucchini, yellow squash, bell peppers,
cheese and salad dressing in a bowl and toss to mix well. Chill, covered, for
2 hours or longer. Mix well before serving.

You may substitute ham, chicken or shrimp for the turkey.

Serves 6

I didn't learn how to play golf until I was 29. While serving in the military I honed my game and was good enough to carry the title "All Army." After 20 years in the army and two tours of Vietnam, I dreamed of playing on the regular Tour, but that dream never came true. I had to wait until I was 50 and qualified for the SENIOR TOUR, but I had some disastrous days early in my career there. One day I was hitting it all over the place—even in a woman's purse—and I needed to find some confidence in my game. Playing with the wonderful pros on the Tour like Ray Floyd and Chi Chi I became more at ease and learned that time and experience do make a difference. In 1996 at Kemper Lakes, I stood up to the challenge and stood in the winner's circle to claim the victory.

LOW-FAT TURKEY LOAF

Walter Morgan

3/4 cup chopped onion
1/4 cup chopped red and/or green bell pepper
1 1/4 pounds lean ground turkey
1/2 cup herb-seasoned stuffing mix or rolled oats
1 egg, lightly beaten
1/2 cup fat-free cream of celery soup
1/2 cup fat-free cream of chicken soup
1/4 teaspoon ground fresh sage
1/2 teaspoon salt
1/2 teaspoon pepper

Combine the onion and bell pepper in a microwave-safe dish. Microwave on High for 2 minutes or until tender; cool.

Combine the onion and pepper mixture with the turkey, stuffing mix, egg, soups, sage, salt and pepper in a bowl and mix well.

Pack into a 5×9-inch loaf pan. Bake at 350 degrees for 1 hour.

Serves 6

Brenda Albus relates that this was New York City-bred Jim's introduction to her family. When they were dating she took him home for a Thanksgiving dinner that her father and brothers had shot that morning. Surrounded by rice fields, Willows is one of the best places in the country for duck and pheasant hunting, but it is an acquired taste, and not a welcome substitute for the traditional turkey that Jim was expecting.

WILD DUCK

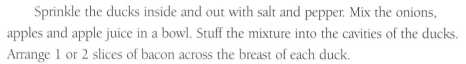

Jim Albus

4 wild ducks or pheasant, cleaned
salt and pepper to taste
2 onions, chopped
2 apples, chopped
1/2 to 1 cup apple juice
4 to 8 slices bacon

Sprinkle the ducks inside and out with salt and pepper. Mix the onions, apples and apple juice in a bowl. Stuff the mixture into the cavities of the ducks. Arrange 1 or 2 slices of bacon across the breast of each duck.

Wrap each duck in heavy-duty foil and place in a roasting pan. Roast at 325 degrees for 3 hours. Skim the pan juices for gravy if desired.

Serves 4

BIRDIES AND BUNKERS • POULTRY • SEAFOOD

I played a lot of golf with my uncle Sam and we had some real interesting times. Once when we were playing in West Virginia a small bobcat came out of the hills and followed us for a while. Sam thought it would be a great idea to catch the bobcat and put it in his golf bag. So we played on for a bit, but we watched the cat out of the corners of our eyes. When the time was right, we captured the cat and put it into his bag. We played the rest of the way with the bobcat yowling in his bag. It was just one of the many ways he found to distract me when we played.

WILD TURKEY

J. C. Snead

Use only the breast portion of wild turkey; the legs are sinewy and tough.

TURKEY
1 wild turkey breast
flour
salt and pepper to taste
1/4 cup (1/2 stick) butter

CREAM GRAVY
1 to 2 tablespoons flour
1 cup milk
salt and pepper to taste

For the turkey, cut the turkey breast into 1×3-inch strips. Coat with a mixture of flour, salt and pepper. Fry in butter in a skillet just until crisp; do not overcook. Remove the turkey to a serving plate.

For the gravy, drain all but 2 tablespoons of the drippings from the skillet. Whisk the flour into the drippings. Cook until bubbly. Add the milk gradually. Cook until thickened, stirring constantly. Season with salt and pepper. Serve with the turkey.

Serves 6

DOVE
....

Bob Eastwood

Special thanks to the Shugarts of Noodle Creek Outfitters for their
real Texas hospitality and our favorite recipe for dove.

12 slices canned or fresh jalapeño pepper
12 dove breasts, boned
12 slices bacon

Place 1 slice of jalapeño pepper on each dove breast and wrap with a slice of bacon; secure with a wooden pick. Arrange in a shallow baking dish. Bake at 200 degrees for 30 minutes.

Place on a grill and grill for 7 to 10 minutes or until the bacon is crisp. You may also broil for 5 to 8 minutes to crisp the bacon.

Serves 6

BIRDIES AND BUNKERS • POULTRY • SEAFOOD

The PGA TOUR added a new tournament in the Wild West in 1981 in Abilene, Texas. I soon discovered such an abundance of dove in the region that I had to really work hard on my golf to keep it from interfering with dove hunting.

Dove hunts are now a tradition here on our own Loop-N-E Ranch. My SENIOR TOUR schedule for September is planned around dove hunting on the ranch and the annual trip to Abilene, about 90 miles west of us.

I grew up in northern California, where my grandfather, Judge W. H. Gilbert instilled in me a love for the outdoors and hunting that continues today, along with my passion for golf. I have had the opportunity to hunt in many places throughout the country, and I always think of my grandfather.

The first time I was invited to hunt in Madison, South Dakota, it was late in the season, and I assumed I might be getting fall or winter temperatures there, so I was prepared for snow. Instead the weather was unusually warm, and I hunted in my shirt sleeves. I was privileged to make a return trip in 2000, and this time I hunted in snow. I've hunted all my life in California, and I saw more pheasant in one day in the snow in South Dakota than I have seen in all those other years!

PHEASANT

. . . .

Bob Eastwood

Thanks to my loyal fans in Madison and especially to my old Army buddy, Roger Southmayd, and Chef Bob Felker for my favorite recipe for cooking pheasant.

boned breasts and thighs of 2 pheasant
salt and pepper to taste
$1/2$ cup honey mustard
2 cups unseasoned bread crumbs
3 tablespoons olive oil

Cut the pheasant breasts and thighs into narrow strips; season with salt and pepper. Roll in the honey mustard and coat with the bread crumbs.

Sauté in the heated olive oil in a heavy skillet until light brown. Drain on paper towels. Place in a baking dish. Bake at 350 degrees for 30 minutes.

Serves 4

During the Buick Open in Grand Blanc, Michigan, many players stayed at the same 12-unit strip motel. My wife Sheri was almost finished cooking her skillet meal when she turned the dial to reheat, and the entire motel went black, even the street sign. The manager brought candles to everyone and, since the "blackout" lasted a while, everyone dined by candlelight that night.

BAKED GROUPER

DeWitt Weaver

2 tablespoons butter, melted
1 small onion, chopped
^{1}/$_2$ cup chopped fresh parsley
6 grouper fillets (about 2 pounds)
^{1}/$_2$ teaspoon salt
^{1}/$_2$ teaspoon pepper
1 cup dry white wine
^{3}/$_4$ cup fine dry bread crumbs
1 tablespoon butter, melted

Drizzle 2 tablespoons butter in a 9×13-inch baking dish. Sprinkle half the onion and parsley into the prepared dish. Sprinkle the fish evenly with the salt and pepper and arrange in the dish. Pour the wine over the top.

Combine the remaining onion and parsley with the bread crumbs in a bowl and mix well. Sprinkle over the fish. Drizzle with 1 tablespoon butter.

Bake at 375 degrees for 22 minutes or until the fish flakes easily with a fork. Broil 5 inches from the heat source until light brown. Garnish with lemon slices and parsley sprigs.

Serves 6

HALIBUT WITH FRESH FRUIT SALSA

Gary McCord

You may substitute salmon or sea bass for the halibut and cherries or peaches for the fruit in this recipe.

FRESH FRUIT SALSA

1/3 cup chopped papaya

1/3 cup pineapple tidbits

1/3 cup chopped seeded Roma tomatoes

1/8 teaspoon minced jalapeño pepper

1/2 teaspoon cilantro

1/4 cup lime juice

HALIBUT

24 ounces halibut fillets

1 cup teriyaki marinade

1 cup Italian salad dressing

For the salsa, combine the papaya, pineapple, tomatoes, jalapeño pepper, cilantro and lime juice in a medium bowl and mix well. Chill, covered, for 3 hours or longer.

For the halibut, combine the fillets with the teriyaki marinade and Italian salad dressing in a sealable plastic bag and turn to coat well. Marinate for 30 minutes or longer; drain.

Grill the halibut for 20 minutes or until it flakes easily with a fork. Serve with the salsa.

Serves 4

Lee Trevino and Tony Jacklin were playing in a match-play tournament after Trevino had beaten Jacklin at the British Open. Tony said to Lee, "I have a lot of friends and family out here today, so I don't want to talk." Lee answered, "That's okay. Just listen."

CEVICHE

Lee Trevino

2 pounds halibut fillets
2 cups (or more) lemon juice
2 cups chopped white onions
16 green olives, sliced
2 hot green serrano peppers, seeded, chopped
3 tomatoes, peeled, seeded, coarsely chopped

chopped cilantro leaves to taste
1/2 cup tomato juice
1/2 cup tomato purée
2 tablespoons Worcestershire sauce
Tabasco sauce to taste
1 tablespoon salt

Cut the halibut into 1/2-inch pieces. Mix with enough lemon juice to cover in a bowl. Marinate in the refrigerator for 6 hours or longer. Combine the onions, green olives, serrano peppers, tomatoes, cilantro, tomato juice, tomato purée, Worcestershire sauce, Tabasco sauce and salt in a bowl and mix well. Drain and discard 1 cup of the lemon juice from the fish. Add the fish and remaining lemon juice to the tomato mixture. Chill in the refrigerator for 8 hours or longer.

Serves 6

There have been many comments and laughs about Bob Charles' eating habits and eating fads over the years, and you never know what he will be eating or taking next. He has produced an avocado out of his jacket pocket at a banquet; even worse, the salad dressing appeared from his other pocket. He is a health enthusiast, and his food supplements include bee pollen, deer velvet, green-lipped mussel extract, bilberry, garlic, ginger and a multi-vitamin. His wife Verity always finds the health food store in each new city.

FLASH-ROASTED SALMON FILLETS

Bob Charles

6 salmon fillets

salt and pepper to taste

1/4 cup fresh lime juice or lemon juice

finely grated lime or lemon zest to taste

1/2 cup Thai sweet chili sauce

Place the salmon fillets in a shallow baking dish lined with baking parchment or foil. Season with salt and pepper. Sprinkle with the lime juice and lime zest; spread with the chili sauce.

Roast at 500 degrees for 7 minutes. Serve with a salad and ciabatta or French bread.

Serves 6

BIRDIES AND BUNKERS • POULTRY • SEAFOOD

Salmon with Ginger and Spring Onion Sauce

....

John Jacobs

Salmon

1/2 cup wine vinegar

2 or 3 sprigs of fresh herbs

24 ounces fresh salmon

Ginger and Spring Onion Sauce

1/4 cup lemon juice

1/4 cup soy sauce

1 tablespoon grated fresh gingerroot

1 tablespoon finely chopped spring onions

For the salmon, measure the amount of water needed to cover the salmon. Combine with the vinegar and fresh herbs in a large saucepan and bring to a boil. Boil for 2 minutes.

Place the salmon gently into the boiling water and return to a boil. Cook for 2 minutes. Cover the saucepan and remove from the heat. Let stand for 45 minutes to 2 hours. Remove the fish from the cooking liquid.

For the sauce, combine the lemon juice, soy sauce, gingerroot and spring onions in a bowl and mix well. Spoon over the salmon to serve.

Serves 4

When Gary Player's daughter Michelle decided to learn to play golf, she signed up for a nine-hole lesson with one of the local golf professionals. She was asked if she had ever had a lesson before and told the pro that her dad had helped her in the past. He told her to disregard all that her dad had told her and to listen to him. A friend taking lessons with her thought that advice might be a little drastic and told the pro that her dad was Gary Player.

Salmon Supreme

. . . .

Gary Player

This is a quick and easy dish to prepare for visitors and makes a colorful presentation.

1 (5-pound) salmon fillet
mayonnaise
herbed salt to taste
grated Parmesan cheese
butter
sliced red bell peppers
lemon juice

Place the salmon fillet in the center of a shallow baking dish. Mix mayonnaise and herbed salt in a bowl and spread in a thin layer over the salmon. Sprinkle generously with Parmesan cheese and dot with butter.

Arrange red bell pepper slices along the sides of the fillet and sprinkle generously with lemon juice. Bake at 380 degrees for 45 minutes.

Serves 10

BIRDIES AND BUNKERS • POULTRY • SEAFOOD

Carolyn Dickson, Bob's wife, was standing near the tee when Bob and Hale Irwin were playing a round. They were teeing off and, just as Hale took his swing, Carolyn dropped her purse. Hale hit the ball out of bounds. Hale was very forgiving, but Bob . . .

SALMON IN FOIL

Bob Dickson

Store the leftover Herb Butter in the refrigerator or freezer until ready to use.

HERB BUTTER	SALMON
1/4 teaspoon tarragon	2 pounds fresh salmon, cut into 4 pieces
1/4 teaspoon basil	1 red bell pepper, julienned
1/8 teaspoon oregano	1 cup snow peas
1/8 teaspoon thyme	1/2 cup julienned jicama
1 teaspoon lemon juice	1/2 cup julienned leeks
1/4 cup (1/2 stick) butter, softened	1 cup julienned carrots

For the butter, combine the tarragon, basil, oregano, thyme, lemon juice and butter in a small bowl and mix well.

For the salmon, cut 4 squares of foil or baking parchment large enough to enclose the salmon pieces. Combine the red pepper, snow peas, jicama, leeks and carrots in a bowl and mix well. Spoon into the centers of the foil squares.

Place one piece of salmon on the vegetables on each square and top with 1 teaspoon of the Herb Butter. Fold the foil to enclose the fish and vegetables.

Place the packets in a baking dish. Bake at 350 degrees for 20 to 25 minutes or until the salmon and vegetables are tender.

Serves 4

GRILLED SHRIMP

Hale Irwin

*Thanks to our daughter Becky for this recipe, which became
an instant family favorite.*

2 pounds peeled shrimp, deveined
1/4 cup olive oil
1 tablespoon minced garlic
1/2 cup seasoned dry bread crumbs
1/4 cup chopped fresh parsley
salt and pepper to taste

Combine the shrimp with the olive oil and garlic in a large bowl and mix well. Add the bread crumbs and parsley and toss to coat the shrimp evenly. Season with salt and pepper.

Thread the shrimp onto sixteen 10- to 12-inch skewers and place on a plate. Chill, covered, in the refrigerator for 30 to 60 minutes.

Grill the shrimp for 2 minutes on each side or just until the shrimp are opaque and the bread crumbs begin to brown.

Serves 8

BIRDIES AND BUNKERS • POULTRY • SEAFOOD

Our first trip to Los Angeles was in 1969, and we stayed at the Temple Motel as recommended by Joyce and Dale Douglass. It was a tiny room with a tiny kitchen. We had so much stuff with us that the maids asked us if we were in the process of moving. Since we had been married less than six months, candlelight was really important. We were eating our meager bowls of chili when Charles Coody walked by and looked in our window. To this day, he asks us when he is going to be invited over for "chili by candlelight."

If nothing else, we learned to be very creative on Tour. I used the shower rod or a golf club for the TV remote control before they came with every TV. There were years that we used towel-lined dresser drawers as baby beds for our daughters.

SPICY SHRIMP

Andy North

1/2 teaspoon dried thyme leaves
1/2 teaspoon dried rosemary leaves
1/8 teaspoon dried oregano leaves
1/2 teaspoon salt
1/2 teaspoon crushed red pepper
1 1/2 teaspoons cayenne pepper
1 teaspoon black pepper
1/2 cup (1 stick) butter
1 1/2 teaspoons minced garlic
1 teaspoon Worcestershire sauce
24 large shrimp, peeled or unpeeled
5 tablespoons butter
1/2 cup beer, at room temperature

Mix the thyme leaves, rosemary leaves, oregano leaves, salt, crushed red pepper, cayenne pepper and black pepper in a small bowl. Combine 1/2 cup butter, garlic, Worcestershire sauce and seasoning mix in a large skillet over high heat. Cook until the butter melts, stirring to mix well.

Add the shrimp and sauté for 2 minutes. Add 5 tablespoons butter and sauté for 2 minutes, stirring gently. Stir in the beer and cook for 1 minute longer, stirring gently.

Serve the shrimp with the spicy sauce in bowls with French bread to dip into the sauce.

Serves 4

SEAFOOD • POULTRY • BIRDIES AND BUNKERS

Our son Jay answered the phone at home one day while I was traveling. Jay called to my wife Mary Rose saying, "Mommy, somebody named Johnny Pott is on the phone."

SHRIMP CREOLE

....

Johnny Pott

Shrimp Creole is best if made the day before and reheated to serve. Add the parsley and green onion tops just before serving.

1 cup flour
1 cup vegetable oil
1 cup chopped celery with leaves
1 cup chopped green bell pepper
2 cups chopped onions
4 garlic cloves, chopped
1 (28-ounce) can diced tomatoes
2 (6-ounce) cans tomato paste
6 cups water
Tabasco sauce to taste
4 teaspoons salt
$1/2$ teaspoon red pepper
$1/2$ teaspoon black pepper
3 pounds shrimp, peeled, deveined
$1/2$ cup chopped fresh parsley
$3/4$ cup chopped green onion tops

Stir the flour into the vegetable oil in a heavy saucepan over low heat. Cook until golden brown, stirring frequently. Add the celery, green pepper, onions and garlic. Cook until the vegetables are tender. Mix the tomatoes and tomato paste and add to the vegetables in the saucepan; mix well.

Stir in the water, Tabasco sauce, salt, red pepper and black pepper. Simmer for 1 hour.

Add the shrimp. Cook for 10 to 15 minutes or just until the shrimp are cooked through. Add the parsley and green onion tops just before serving. Serve over rice. Add a salad and French bread.

Serves 8 to 10

TORTELLINI AND SHRIMP

Terry Dill

1 (16-ounce) package refrigerated cheese-filled tortellini
$1/3$ cup butter
1 pound fresh peeled shrimp
1 shallot or 3 green onions, chopped
2 teaspoons basil, or 2 tablespoons chopped fresh basil
$1/2$ cup grated Parmesan cheese

Cook the pasta using the package directions; rinse and drain.

Melt the butter in a large skillet over medium heat. Add the shrimp, shallot and basil. Sauté for 5 minutes, stirring constantly.

Add the pasta and Parmesan cheese to the shrimp. Cook until heated through, tossing to mix well.

Serves 4

CALAMARI UMIDO

Gary Player

1 (500-gram) can Italian tomatoes

1 medium onion, finely chopped

1 carrot, finely chopped

1 rib celery, finely chopped

1 garlic clove, crushed

2 tablespoons extra-virgin olive oil

1 kilogram calamari, sliced into rings

¹/4 cup white wine

500 grams sliced mushrooms, sautéed

1 bunch spinach, cooked, chopped

salt and pepper to taste

cooked tagliolini

cream to taste

Combine the tomatoes, onion, carrot and celery in a bowl and mix well. Sauté the garlic in the olive oil in a large heavy skillet until aromatic. Add the calamari and sauté for 2 minutes or until light brown. Add the wine and the tomato mixture. Cook for 2 minutes. Stir in the mushrooms, spinach, salt and pepper. Cook until heated through. Panfry the tagliolini in a skillet until golden brown. Add the cream. Serve the calamari over the tagliolini.

Refer to the Metric Conversion Chart on page 215 for measurement equivalents.

Serves 8

ON THE GREEN

SALADS • SIDE DISHES

BLUEBERRY GELATIN SALAD

Tom Kite

*This is Byron and Louise Nelson's recipe, prepared for the wives of the
SENIOR TOUR members at a luncheon at their ranch.*

1 (20-ounce) can crushed pineapple
1 (15-ounce) can blueberries
8 ounces cream cheese, softened
1 (3-ounce) package berry blue gelatin
1 (3-ounce) package red raspberry gelatin
1 cup chopped pecans

Drain the pineapple and blueberries, reserving the juice. Combine
1 tablespoon of the reserved juice with the cream cheese in a bowl and mix
well. Combine the remaining juice with enough boiling water to measure 4 cups.
Dissolve the berry blue gelatin and red raspberry gelatin in the juice mixture
in a large bowl. Add the pineapple, blueberries, cream cheese and pecans and mix
well. Spoon into a gelatin mold and chill, covered, until set.

Serves 8 to 10

ON THE GREEN • SALADS • SIDE DISHES

I was tired of staying in bad hotels, so I decided to find out where Chi Chi Rodriguez and Lee Trevino were staying at the next tournament. I knew that they had played there and would know their way around, so I asked the housing chairman to book me a room "where Chi Chi is."

After arriving we picked up our courtesy car and directions to the hotel. We drove for more than 45 minutes before arriving at our destination to see that it was "the pits!" I called the tournament office and explained that there must be some mistake because Rodriguez would not stay in a place like this. The tournament director said, "Who said anything about Rodriguez? I thought you wanted to stay near a Chi Chi's Restaurant."

CURRIED APPLE AND CELERY SALAD

John Jacobs

CURRY DRESSING
1/3 cup sour cream
2 tablespoons mayonnaise
2 tablespoons orange juice
1 teaspoon curry powder

SALAD
2 apples, chopped
4 ribs celery, chopped
3/4 cup toasted slivered almonds
3/4 cup raisins
1 tablespoon chopped parsley

For the dressing, combine the sour cream, mayonnaise, orange juice and curry powder in a bowl and mix well.

For the salad, combine the apples, celery, almonds, raisins and parsley in a bowl and toss to mix. Add the dressing and mix gently. Chill, covered, until ready to serve.

Serves 4

A reporter once came to the pool area of the hotel to interview several of the wives who were playing bridge, when my three-year-old daughter Kelly came over carrying a little purse. The reporter asked what was inside, so she opened it and showed the reporter a deck of cards and poker chips inside! Kelly explained to the reporter that the kids wouldn't let her play gin. Somehow that became the news story for the paper.

COOL CRANBERRY AND APPLE SQUARES

Jim Colbert

*This makes a colorful holiday salad that can be prepared
up to two weeks in advance.*

3 cups fresh whole cranberries
4 large red apples, cored, chopped
1/2 cup sugar
1 (7-ounce) jar marshmallow creme
8 ounces light whipped topping

Combine the cranberries and unpeeled apples in a food processor and process until finely chopped. Combine the chopped fruit, sugar and marshmallow creme in a bowl and mix well. Let stand, covered, for 3 to 4 hours.

Fold the whipped topping into the fruit mixture. Spoon into a 9×13-inch dish and freeze, covered, until firm. Remove from the freezer 20 minutes prior to serving. Cut into squares and serve on lettuce lined plates.

Serves 14 to 16

ON THE GREEN • SALADS • SIDE DISHES

Our granddaughter Ashley was working on learning her "plusses," or addition, and her "take-aways," or subtraction. She told her mom that she could turn on the television and check grandpa's score all by herself. She diligently watched the ticker tape at the bottom of the screen until she saw my name, then ran upstairs and reported that grandpa was "take-away two"—her version of two under par.

RASPBERRY GELATIN SALAD
....
Bruce Summerhays

This is dressy enough for company yet great for everyday or family gatherings.

1 (6-ounce) package raspberry gelatin
2$\frac{1}{2}$ cups boiling water
1 (12-ounce) package frozen raspberries
1 (8-ounce) can crushed pineapple
1 banana, sliced
$\frac{1}{2}$ cup chopped pecans (optional)
sour cream or whipped topping

Dissolve the raspberry gelatin in the boiling water in a bowl. Add the raspberries, undrained pineapple, banana and pecans and mix will. Pour into a 9×13-inch dish and chill, covered, until set. Cut into squares and garnish with sour cream or whipped cream.

Serves 6 to 8

My daughter Holly caddied for me at a Hooters Tour Event in Columbia, South Carolina. On the third hole of the first day, a bee flew up her shorts and stung her. The officials had to take her to the hospital since she is allergic to bee stings. She has never caddied for me since.

FROZEN FRUIT SALAD

Walter Hall

1 (10-ounce) jar cherries, drained
1 (15-ounce) can crushed pineapple, drained
8 ounces cream cheese, softened
3 tablespoons mayonnaise
1 (16-ounce) package miniature marshmallows
1 cup chopped pecans or English walnuts
1/2 pint whipping cream, whipped

Cut each cherry into halves. Combine the cherries, pineapple, cream cheese, mayonnaise, marshmallows and pecans in a large bowl and mix well. Fold in the whipped cream. Spoon into a 9×13-inch serving dish and freeze, covered, until firm.

Serves 12

ON THE GREEN • SALADS • SIDE DISHES

During my first years on the Tour, my youngest daughter, Andrea, loved to hang out with the caddies. At three she was already the life of the party. She would dance and dance, living up to the "Born to Boogie" T-shirt she sported. Between the dancing and the T-shirt, she became "Boogie." Twenty years later she's outgrown the T-shirt, but the nickname "Boogs" remains.

CREAMY FRUIT SALAD

Andy North

3/4 (4-ounce) package French vanilla instant pudding mix
1 cup sour cream
2 (8-ounce) cans mandarin oranges, drained
1 (20-ounce) can pineapple tidbits, drained
2 cups miniature marshmallows

Combine the pudding mix and the sour cream in a bowl and mix well. Add the mandarin oranges and pineapple and stir gently to mix. Chill, covered, for 8 hours. Stir in the marshmallows just before serving.

Serves 6

TWENTY-FOUR HOUR SALAD

Jim Ahern

1 (20-ounce) can pineapple chunks
1 pound red seedless grapes
1 pound white cherries
1 (16-ounce) package miniature marshmallows
1 pound pecans, chopped
1 pint heavy cream
juice of 1 lemon
2 tablespoons sugar
4 egg yolks

Drain the pineapple, reserving 1/4 cup of the juice. Combine the pineapple, grapes, cherries, marshmallows, pecans and heavy cream in a large bowl and mix gently.

Combine the reserved juice, lemon juice, sugar and egg yolks in a saucepan. Cook over medium heat until thickened, stirring constantly. Remove from heat and cool to room temperature.

Pour over the fruit mixture and toss gently to coat. Chill, covered, for up to 24 hours.

Serves 12 to 16

ON THE GREEN • SALADS • SIDE DISHES

AVOCADO AND CRAB BOATS

....

David Lundstrom

4 firm ripe avocados

lemon juice

1/2 teaspoon salt

1 (7-ounce) can crab meat, drained

3 hard-cooked eggs, chopped

1/3 cup chopped celery

2 tablespoons chopped pimentos

1 tablespoon chopped onion

1/2 cup mayonnaise

3 tablespoons bread crumbs

1 teaspoon butter, melted

3 tablespoons slivered almonds

Cut each avocado into halves and remove the seed; do not peel. Brush the cut side of each avocado with the lemon juice. Sprinkle with the salt.

Combine the crab meat, eggs, celery, pimentos, onion and mayonnaise in a bowl and mix well. Combine the bread crumbs and butter in a bowl and mix well. Spoon the crab meat mixture into the avocado halves. Top with the bread crumbs.

Arrange the filled avocado halves in a baking pan. Bake at 350 degrees for 10 minutes. Sprinkle with the almonds. Bake for 5 minutes longer.

Serves 8

BROCCOLI SALAD

Bob Dickson

SALAD
1 (3-ounce) package oriental-style ramen noodles, crumbled
1/4 cup sliced almonds
2 tablespoons butter, softened
1 (16-ounce) package broccoli slaw

SWEET-AND-SOUR DRESSING
1/2 cup vegetable oil
1/4 cup sugar
1/4 cup red wine vinegar
1 tablespoon soy sauce
1/4 teaspoon salt
1/8 teaspoon pepper

For the salad, set aside the flavor packet from the ramen noodles. Combine the noodles, almonds and butter in a bowl and mix well. Spread the mixture in a baking pan. Broil until lightly toasted. Cool to room temperature. Combine with the broccoli slaw in a bowl and toss to mix.

For the dressing, combine the seasonings from the flavor packet, oil, sugar, vinegar, soy sauce, salt and pepper in a bowl and whisk until blended.

Pour the dressing over the salad and toss to coat. Chill, covered, for 1 hour before serving.

Serves 6

Many of the SENIOR PGA TOUR players have continued their golfing careers as an extension of the regular PGA TOUR. Others have taken different paths to the SENIOR TOUR, with various careers prior to becoming a part of the Tour. Some of those careers include: author, banker, cattle rancher, farmer, football player, hair stylist, jeweler, mayor, movie consultant, professional singer, professional tennis player, real estate developer, school teacher, and sports reporter and anchorman.

LEFT TO RIGHT: Brian "Bruno" Henning, Carolyn Dickson, Valerie Henning, Jim Colbert, Marcia Colbert, Bob Dickson

Chinese Cabbage Salad

Bruce Fleisher, Bob Murphy and Jack Nicklaus

Oriental Dressing
3/4 cup canola oil

1/2 cup sugar

1/4 cup white vinegar

2 tablespoons soy sauce

Salad
1 (2-ounce) package sliced or slivered almonds

3 to 4 tablespoons sesame seeds

1 to 1 1/2 (3-ounce) packages ramen noodles, crushed

1/4 cup (1/2 stick) butter

1 large head Napa cabbage, shredded,

or 2 to 3 bunches bok choy, chopped

4 green onions, chopped

1 (8-ounce) can mandarin oranges, drained (optional)

For the dressing, combine the canola oil, sugar, vinegar and soy sauce in a small saucepan. Cook over low heat until the sugar dissolves and the mixture is slightly thickened, stirring constantly. Chill, covered, until ready to use.

For the salad, sauté the almonds, sesame seeds and crushed ramen noodles in the butter in a skillet until lightly browned. Stir in the seasonings from the flavor packets. Drain on a paper towel. Combine the cabbage, green onions and mandarin oranges in a large bowl and toss gently.

To serve, sprinkle the noodle mixture over the cabbage. Pour the dressing over the salad and toss gently to combine.

You may add 2 1/2 cups of chopped cooked chicken or shrimp for a main-dish salad.

Serves 4

In 1977 a reporter asked my two-year-old son Jay, "Where do you live, little boy?"
He responded, "In a hotel."

CHOPPED SALAD

Doug Tewell

We think Martinique Poppy Seed Salad Dressing is the best for this salad.

1 small head red-leaf lettuce, chopped
1 small head romaine, chopped
$1/2$ cup finely chopped celery
1 cup grated Parmesan cheese
$1/4$ cup unsalted sunflower kernels
1 tablespoon McCormick Salad Supreme
freshly ground pepper
1 (11-ounce) can mandarin oranges, drained
poppy seed salad dressing to taste

Combine the lettuce, celery, Parmesan cheese, sunflower kernels, Salad Supreme, pepper and mandarin oranges in a large bowl and toss gently. Pour the salad dressing over the salad and toss gently to combine.

You may substitute $1/2$ cup toasted slivered almonds for the sunflower kernels or $1/2$ to 1 cup sliced fresh strawberries for the mandarin oranges, or you may use a combination of the fruits.

Serves 4 to 6

CARAMELIZED SHALLOT SALAD

Andy North

2 pounds shallots
1 cup vegetable broth
2 tablespoons brown sugar
3/4 cup balsamic vinegar
1/2 teaspoon pepper
1/2 teaspoon salt
2 garlic cloves, minced
3/4 cup olive oil
romaine lettuce, torn
Bibb lettuce, torn
8 ounces bleu cheese, crumbled

Combine the shallots, vegetable broth and brown sugar in a large skillet. Cook, covered, over medium heat for 30 minutes or until the shallots are tender, stirring occasionally. Reduce the heat and simmer, uncovered, for 20 minutes or until golden brown, stirring frequently. Spoon the shallots into a large glass dish.

Whisk together the vinegar, pepper, salt and garlic in a bowl. Stir in the olive oil slowly. Reserve 1/2 cup of the mixture. Pour the remaining mixture over the shallots. Chill, covered, for 8 hours.

Toss the lettuce with the reserved vinegar mixture in a bowl. Arrange the lettuce on serving plates. Drain the shallots and spoon over the lettuce. Sprinkle with the bleu cheese.

Serves 10

ON THE GREEN • SALADS • SIDE DISHES

Almost every wife that travels on Tour has a "we stick." This is a unique invention consisting of an umbrella with a handle that becomes a seat to rest on during the tournament. The wives say that as "we" rest upon the seats, "we" can see the shots and putts that "we" make during each round. Susan North was sitting on her "we" stick when Andy hit a ball into her elbow on the fly with a one-iron, and flipped her off her seat.

Andy North with daughters Nichole and Andrea

One of my favorite tournaments is the TransAmerica Senior Classic held every year in Napa Valley, California. You may think it is because of the beautiful crisp morning walks, wide open spaces, soft rolling hills or dewy green fairways of the Silverado Resort. It is actually the sunny afternoons at the Jenkins' small boutique family vineyard at Wing Canyon on Mount Veeder. There we enjoy the great wine that is made there and festive dinners with my brother Bill and his wife Kathy before the tournament starts. It is also where little TJ became a twinkle in our eyes on a starry night in 1999 and where he was born in 2000. Wing Canyon Cabernet Sauvignon holds a special place in our hearts.

BLEU CHEESE AND LETTUCE SALAD

Tom Jenkins

The easy and quick five-minute preparation time on this salad allows for more time to visit with family and guests.

2 cups extra-virgin olive oil
1 cup 20-year old balsamic vinegar
2 cups crumbled bleu cheese
1 head iceberg lettuce, quartered
freshly ground pepper

Whisk together the olive oil and vinegar in a bowl. Stir in the bleu cheese. Place the lettuce on 4 serving plates. Pour the bleu cheese dressing over the lettuce. Sprinkle generously with pepper.

Serves 4

ON THE GREEN • SALADS • SIDE DISHES

Vivienne Player can boast about a round of golf she had while playing in Johannesburg that her husband Gary has not equaled. She had two holes-in-one in one round and missed her third by only an inch!

INSALATA PIEDMONTESE

Gary Player

300 grams sun-dried tomatoes, chopped
olive oil
1 aubergine, thinly sliced
500 grams mushrooms
100 grams capers, drained
1 bunch butter lettuce
1 bunch mixed lettuce
balsamic vinegar to taste
salt to taste
1/4 cup roasted pine nuts
Parmesan cheese shavings to taste
freshly ground pepper to taste

Soak the tomatoes in olive oil to taste in a bowl. Brush both sides of the aubergine slices with olive oil. Grill the aubergine on a flat grill until tender, turning once. Sauté the mushrooms in olive oil in a skillet until tender but firm.

Combine the tomatoes, mushrooms and capers in a bowl and stir gently. Combine the butter lettuce, mixed lettuce, balsamic vinegar, olive oil and salt in a bowl and toss gently to mix.

Heap the lettuce onto serving plates. Top each plate with 1 tablespoon of the tomato mixture. Sprinkle with the pine nuts. Arrange 5 slices of the aubergine around each salad. Sprinkle with the Parmesan cheese and pepper.

Refer to the Metric Conversion Chart on page 215 for measurement equivalents.

Serves 4

GRILLED PORTOBELLO SALAD WITH AVOCADO AND GOAT CHEESE

Raymond Floyd

2 tablespoons white wine

1 tablespoon minced garlic

1 tablespoon olive oil

$3/4$ teaspoon kosher salt

$1/2$ teaspoon freshly ground pepper

$1/2$ teaspoon oregano

4 large portobello mushroom caps

1 yellow tomato, thinly sliced

1 avocado, thinly sliced

1 roasted red bell pepper, thinly sliced

4 ounces fresh goat cheese, thinly sliced

1 head frisée lettuce, torn

Combine the wine, garlic, olive oil, salt, pepper and oregano in a shallow dish and mix well. Marinate the mushrooms in the wine mixture for 30 minutes. Grill the mushrooms over medium-hot coals for 3 minutes or until cooked through, turning frequently.

Arrange the grilled mushrooms in a baking pan. Top each with some of the tomato, avocado, red pepper and goat cheese. Broil until the cheese is melted and light brown.

Arrange the lettuce on serving plates. Top each with a prepared mushroom.

Serves 4

ON THE GREEN • SALADS • SIDE DISHES

I played my first Masters in 1965. I shot 68 the first day and was 3 shots behind the leader, Gary Player. On the second round I checked my pairing and discovered that I would be playing with Arnold Palmer. On Friday I arrived at the golf course two hours before my starting time to avoid any possible traffic and to be totally relaxed and prepared for the round. When I got to my locker, there were dozens of telegrams and messages from my friends, and writers stopping me for interviews. I got so caught up in the moment that when I arrived on the practice tee, I looked down to discover that I was still wearing my street shoes. I sheepishly rushed back to the locker room, changed my shoes, and proceeded to shoot 81 and miss the cut!

This was also the year that Jack Nicklaus shot 271 to break Ben Hogan's record by 3 shots. It was 11 years later, in 1976, that I also shot 271 to tie Jack's record and win my first Masters! My wife Maria says that the first tournament that I took her to was the Masters, and she thought they were all going to be like that!

My wife and I have been traveling on the Tour for many, many years. It's always a challenge for people to remember names from year to year. My wife has come up with a great solution for us. She just tells people we're "Normal." That's Norma and Al, happy to be out on the Tour.

DEVILED POTATO SALAD

Al Kelley

2 pounds potatoes
2 hard-cooked eggs
1/2 cup mayonnaise
1/3 cup dijonnaise mustard
1 tablespoon cider vinegar
1/2 teaspoon salt
1/2 teaspoon sugar
1/2 cup chopped celery
1/3 cup chopped red onion
1 tablespoon pickle relish

Combine the potatoes with enough water to cover in a saucepan. Bring to a boil and boil just until tender. Drain and cool the potatoes. Peel and cut into 1/2-inch pieces. Chop the eggs into 1/2-inch pieces.

Combine the mayonnaise, dijonnaise, cider vinegar, salt and sugar in a bowl and stir until blended. Add the celery, red onion and pickle relish and mix well. Add the potatoes and eggs and mix gently. Serve immediately or chill, covered, for 1 hour.

Serves 8

ON THE GREEN • SALADS • SIDE DISHES

Our children and grandchildren have their own version of what golf is all about. My son William brought his family to the Transamerica Tournament in Napa, California. At dinner the night before the tournament, three-year-old Whitney asked me to go to the golf course the next day with her and her daddy. Her daddy explained to her that they would be watching me play in the tournament, as that was his job. After a moment of thought, Whitney replied, "You sillies. Golf isn't a job."

On another occasion, two-year-old Joseph was found hopping on the patio and chanting his favorite nursery rhyme: "Jack be Nicklaus, Jack be quick, Jack jump over the candlestick."

FROG EYE SALAD

Bruce Summerhays

This family favorite goes back many years. Some people call it the Summerhays Special.

1¾ cups pineapple juice

1 tablespoon lemon juice

1 cup sugar

2 tablespoons flour

½ teaspoon salt

2 eggs

1 package acini de pepe, cooked

2 (11-ounce) cans mandarin oranges, drained

2 (20-ounce) cans pineapple chunks, drained

grapes, strawberries, melons to taste

8 ounces whipped topping

Combine the pineapple juice, lemon juice, sugar, flour, salt and eggs in a medium saucepan. Cook over medium heat until thickened, stirring constantly.

Combine the juice mixture and pasta in a large bowl and mix gently. Chill, covered, for 8 hours. Stir in the fruit and whipped topping.

Serves 12

I always look forward to playing Long Island as I have a good friend there who caddies for me. He is seventy years old but keeps himself in great shape, and I enjoy having him on my bag. One year it got to be too much for him, and on the 17th hole he said that he was just too tired to go on. So I took my clubs out of the bag, and he carried an empty bag while I carried my own clubs for the final two holes. What are good friends for?

LUNCHEON PASTA SALAD

Tom Wargo

8 ounces your favorite pasta, cooked, cooled
1 (8-ounce) can mandarin oranges, drained
1/2 cup chopped Granny Smith apple
1/4 cup frozen peas, thawed
1/4 cup chopped pecans
1/2 cup burgundy poppy seed dressing
1 package fresh spinach leaves, washed, drained

Combine the pasta, mandarin oranges, apple, peas and pecans in a large bowl and toss to mix. Add the dressing and mix gently.

Line a serving bowl with the spinach leaves. Spoon the salad into the prepared bowl.

Serves 8

ON THE GREEN • SALADS • SIDE DISHES

Some of our Pro-Am tee times can be very early in the morning, so we try to sneak out of the room to let our wives sleep in. Some of us do this better than others. If you check out our shoes and socks on some of these mornings you will find that we have been known to put on a black sock and a blue sock with a brown shoe and a black shoe. Perfect we're not, but we do try hard!

BEST-EVER EGG SALAD

Miller Barber

12 hard-cooked eggs, chopped
1/2 onion, minced
1 cup shredded sharp Cheddar cheese
1/2 cup mayonnaise
2 teaspoons lemon juice
1 teaspoon salt
3/4 teaspoon curry powder

Combine the eggs, onion, Cheddar cheese, mayonnaise, lemon juice, salt and curry powder in a food processor and pulse until well mixed. Serve as a salad or as a filling for sandwiches.

Serves 6

Playing on the European Tour can be an interesting adventure. At one tournament, the golfer's ride dropped him in the center of the town in which the event was held. He had no hotel and no idea where to stay. While he was standing there wondering what to do, a European player came by, recognized him, and offered him a ride. He was taken to a bed and breakfast near the course, a perfect place to stay, since he didn't have a car. The next morning he set out on foot for the golf course with his clubs on his back. He climbed a fence and started across the pasture separating him from the golf course. When he was halfway across, he saw a bull out of the corner of his eye! He ran for the far fence, threw his clubs over it, and dove under. Every day that week he had to outrun the bull to get to the golf course.

ROASTED ASPARAGUS

Terry Dill

1¹/₂ pounds fresh asparagus, trimmed
1¹/₂ tablespoons olive oil
salt to taste
freshly ground pepper to taste
1¹/₂ tablespoons olive oil
1 tablespoon fresh lemon juice
1 teaspoon grated lemon zest

Arrange the asparagus in a baking dish. Drizzle with 1¹/₂ tablespoons olive oil. Sprinkle with the salt and pepper. Roast at 450 degrees for 10 minutes or until the asparagus is tender. Drizzle with 1¹/₂ tablespoons olive oil and the lemon juice. Sprinkle with the lemon zest.

Serves 4

ON THE GREEN • SALADS • SIDE DISHES

I think that vegetables are truly one of nature's special gifts to mankind, for they offer so much in color, taste, nutrition, decoration and cooking options. I have the "green thumb" in the family and grow vegetables and flowers at our Lake LBJ home. My vegetable garden measures 40 feet by 50 feet, so we always have an abundance of fresh vegetables for our table and to share with our friends and neighbors. Our grandchildren love to go to the garden with "Pickle," their nickname for me, and pick the vegetables for every meal, and we have learned that they will eat almost anything that they pick!

BROCCOLI CASSEROLE

. . . .

Bruce Fleisher and Bob Murphy

2 (10-ounce) packages frozen broccoli florets
1 (10-ounce) package frozen broccoli cuts
2 eggs
1 (10-ounce) can cream of broccoli soup
1 cup sour cream
2 cups shredded Cheddar cheese
salt and pepper to taste
1 cup shredded Cheddar cheese
butter crackers, crushed
butter

Cook the broccoli using the package directions; drain. Beat the eggs in a large bowl. Add the soup and sour cream and mix until blended. Stir in 2 cups Cheddar cheese, salt, pepper and broccoli.

Spoon into a greased 9×13-inch baking dish. Sprinkle with 1 cup Cheddar cheese and cracker crumbs. Dot with butter. Bake at 350 degrees for 45 minutes. Let stand for a few minutes before serving.

You may substitute cream of mushroom soup for the cream of broccoli soup and mayonnaise for the sour cream if desired.

Serves 8 to 10

ON THE GREEN • SALADS • SIDE DISHES

In 1977 at the Colonial Golf Tournament I hit a wild drive to the right and heard a lot of yelling where the ball landed. Everyone hurried down and found a large group of people gathered around a very shaken marshal. The ball had somehow landed inside his pants and lodged next to his most private parts. Officials arrived and that is when the fun began. The first official told the marshal he had to drop his pants. The second official told me that I had to play my ball where it landed. Finally, believe it or not, I had to reach into the poor man's pants and retrieve the ball myself. Rules state that the player must identify his ball. Everyone but the marshal was very amused. The story made as many headlines as Al Geiberger shooting 59 the same day!

Hotel laundries do not handle golf shirts very well, so I have ventured into a laundromat occasionally while on Tour. I once tried to do the laundry in Florida, but had to call my wife in New Zealand for instructions on cleaning up the flood I had created. My wife suspects that laundry is one of the reasons I like her to travel with me.

ROASTED RED PEPPERS

Bob Charles

Roasted red peppers are a delicious and colorful addition to beef or lamb.

2 red bell peppers
4 basil leaves
2 tomatoes, cut into quarters
chopped garlic to taste
2 teaspoons brown sugar
balsamic vinegar to taste
2 tablespoons olive oil

Cut the bell peppers into halves lengthwise, leaving the stems intact. Remove the seeds. Place a basil leaf, 2 tomato quarters and garlic in each bell pepper half. Sprinkle with the brown sugar. Drizzle with balsamic vinegar and olive oil.

Place the prepared bell peppers in a shallow baking dish lined with baking parchment. Roast at 350 degrees for 60 minutes on the top oven shelf.

Serves 4

ON THE GREEN • SALADS • SIDE DISHES

CHUCKWAGON HOMINY

Bob Eastwood

This is a great side dish with dove and pheasant. Cowboy cook and poet Steve Rogers of Stamford, Texas, made this dish for us in an iron Dutch oven buried in a fire pit in the ground at a real cowboy cookout! It is also very good made in a traditional oven.

2 (15-ounce) cans white or golden hominy, drained

1 (15-ounce) can diced tomatoes with green chiles

1 (4-ounce) can sliced black olives, drained

1 (2-ounce) jar chopped pimentos, drained

4 ounces cream cheese, cubed

3 cups shredded four-cheese blend

salt and pepper to taste

1 cup sour cream

Combine the hominy, tomatoes, olives, pimentos, cream cheese, four-cheese blend, salt and pepper in a large bowl and mix well. Spoon into a baking dish. Bake at 350 degrees for 25 to 35 minutes or until bubbly. Serve with the sour cream.

Serves 10

Bob and Dell Eastwood

Holiday Potato Casserole

Bruno Henning

3 pounds potatoes
1/2 cup (1 stick) butter or margarine
6 ounces cream cheese
1/2 cup shredded Cheddar cheese
1 (2-ounce) jar pimentos, drained
1/4 cup milk
1 teaspoon salt
1 small green bell pepper, chopped
1 bunch green onions, chopped
1/2 cup grated Parmesan cheese
1/2 cup shredded Cheddar cheese

Cook the potatoes in enough water to cover in a saucepan until tender; drain. Mash the potatoes using a potato masher. Add the butter and cream cheese and beat until smooth. Add 1/2 cup Cheddar cheese, pimentos, milk, salt, bell pepper, green onions and Parmesan cheese and mix well.

Spoon into a greased 2-quart baking dish. Bake at 350 degrees for 40 minutes. Sprinkle with 1/2 cup Cheddar cheese and bake 5 minutes longer or until the cheese is melted.

You may prepare this casserole in advance and chill until time to bake.

Serves 8

On The Green • Salads • Side Dishes

GARLIC AND BASIL MASHED POTATOES

Deane Beman

10 garlic cloves

3 tablespoons olive oil

9 medium potatoes, peeled, chopped

salt to taste

3/4 cup sour cream

1/4 cup grated Parmesan cheese

1/4 teaspoon salt

1/4 cup (about) milk

1/4 cup packed fresh basil leaves, chopped

3 tablespoons grated Parmesan cheese

fresh basil leaves (optional)

Place the garlic cloves in a small soufflé dish or ramekin. Drizzle the olive oil over the garlic. Bake at 350 degrees for 20 minutes or until the garlic is tender. Cool to room temperature. Press the garlic from the skins, reserving the oil.

Combine the potatoes with enough salted water to cover in a saucepan. Bring to a boil and cook for 20 to 25 minutes or until tender; drain. Spoon the potatoes into a large bowl.

Beat the potatoes with a mixer at low speed. Add the sour cream, 1/4 cup Parmesan cheese, roasted garlic, reserved garlic oil and 1/4 teaspoon salt. Beat in the milk until fluffy, adding additional milk if necessary. Stir in 1/4 cup basil. Spoon into a greased 2-quart baking dish. Chill, covered, for up to 24 hours.

Bake, covered, at 325 degrees for 45 minutes. Stir the potatoes and sprinkle with 3 tablespoons Parmesan cheese. Bake at 325 degrees for 30 to 45 minutes longer or until heated through. Garnish with basil leaves.

Serves 12

I was playing in a team event with Bobby Nichols, who had promised his wife Nancy a mink coat if we won. I told my wife Donna that was not part of our deal. We went on to win and Nancy got her mink. Later, while playing in a West Coast tournament, we stayed with friends who sold minks, and I got a lesson on how to tell their value. After winning the tournament on Saturday, I walked in to find a perfect mink hanging on the chair with an opened box beneath it. Knowing the value of the mink now, I almost had a heart attack. Donna laughed, for it was our friend's mink! Warning: Do not do this if your husband is on the SENIOR TOUR!

SMASHING MASHED POTATOES

George Archer

Eat and enjoy! Don't worry about the calories; there are millions!

12 potatoes, peeled, cut into quarters
$1/2$ cup (1 stick) butter
2 cups sour cream
1 tablespoon dillweed
milk

Cook the potatoes in enough water to cover in a large saucepan for 40 minutes; drain. Combine the potatoes with the butter, sour cream and dillweed in a large bowl and beat until smooth adding milk until of the desired consistency.

Serves 12 to 15

ON THE GREEN   •   SALADS   •   SIDE DISHES

Every New Year's Day, we eat black-eyed peas to bring us good luck in the coming year. This is a Southern tradition. We have taken our cans of black-eyed peas with us throughout the country to be heated in many five-star restaurants so that we could continue our tradition.

STUFFED YELLOW SQUASH

Dale Douglass

3 medium yellow squash	1/4 cup grated Parmesan cheese
1/2 teaspoon minced garlic	1/3 cup soft bread crumbs
1/2 onion, chopped	1 tablespoon chopped parsley
2 tablespoons butter	

Cut the squash into halves lengthwise. Scoop out the pulp, leaving 1/4-inch thick squash shells; reserve the pulp. Cook the shells in boiling water in a saucepan for 3 minutes; drain. Cook the garlic and onion in the butter in a skillet until tender. Add the reserved pulp and cook until heated through, stirring frequently. Stir in the Parmesan cheese, bread crumbs and parsley.

Spoon the mixture into the squash shells. Arrange the stuffed shells in a baking dish. Bake at 350 degrees for 30 minutes.

Serves 6

Dale and Joyce Douglass

I was playing in a tournament in Florida and had come from behind to go ahead of Gary Player when, on the 18th hole, it started to rain very hard. In those days, the round did not count unless everyone finished. After a three-hour delay, it was decided to back a linen truck up to the 18th green and put towels all over the green to soak up the water so the last group could finish the round.

SQUASH AND ZUCCHINI NOODLES

Bob Murphy

Both adults and kids love this quick and easy dish.

2 tablespoons olive oil
2 tablespoons finely chopped garlic
2 tablespoons finely chopped onion
2 medium to large yellow squash, thinly sliced
2 medium to large zucchini, thinly sliced
1/4 cup chicken broth
Cavender's Greek seasoning to taste
pepper to taste
1/4 cup grated Parmesan cheese
2 tablespoons chopped parsley

Heat the olive oil in a skillet over high heat. Add the garlic, onion, yellow squash and zucchini and cook for 45 seconds to 1 minute, stirring constantly. Add the chicken broth and cook for 2 minutes longer, stirring constantly. Sprinkle with the Greek seasoning and pepper. Spoon into a serving dish. Add the Parmesan cheese and parsley and toss gently to mix. Serve immediately.

Serves 4

ON THE GREEN • SALADS • SIDE DISHES

After I won the 1982 U.S. Amateur at the Country Club, some reporters, tired of interviewing me, decided to ask my wife Betty to tell them something they didn't already know about me. After pondering the question for a few moments, Betty answered, "What can you say about beige?" Actually, I love to tell jokes, and most of the time I am the one who laughs the loudest at the punch line. One of my favorite sayings—a typical "Jayism"—is "Of all the people I've met in the whole wide world, you're one." I enjoy entertaining my fellow pros, their wives and just about anyone else who will listen.

ZUCCHINI AND CORN

Jay Sigel

2 to 3 ears fresh corn

1/2 cup (1 stick) butter

4 to 5 slices large Bermuda onion

1 medium or 2 small zucchini, thinly sliced

1/2 teaspoon sugar

1 cup freshly grated Parmesan cheese

salt and pepper to taste

Cut the corn off the cobs. Melt the butter in a skillet. Add the onion and zucchini and sauté until tender-crisp. Stir in the corn and sugar and heat through. Sprinkle with the Parmesan cheese, salt and pepper.

Serves 4 to 6

SWEET POTATO CASSEROLE

Walter Hall

3 to 4 cups mashed cooked sweet potatoes

2 eggs, beaten

$^1/_3$ stick margarine, softened

1 cup sugar

$^1/_2$ cup evaporated milk

1 teaspoon sherry or almond extract

1 teaspoon imitation butter flavoring

1 teaspoon coconut extract

1 cup packed light brown sugar

$^1/_3$ cup flour

$^1/_3$ cup margarine, melted

1 cup chopped pecans

Combine the sweet potatoes, eggs, $^1/_3$ stick margarine, sugar, evaporated milk, sherry and flavorings in a large mixing bowl and beat until blended. Spoon into a 9×13-inch baking dish.

Combine the brown sugar, flour, $^1/_3$ cup melted margarine and pecans in a bowl and mix well. Sprinkle over the prepared sweet potatoes. Bake at 350 degrees for 25 to 35 minutes or until golden brown.

Serves 10

O N   T H E   G R E E N   •   S A L A D S   •   S I D E   D I S H E S

While playing in the first round in the Asian Tour in Calcutta, India, in 1995, my playing partner hit his 17th tee shot in the left rough. The shot landed in a cow pile—a fresh cow pile, no doubt, since cows are sacred and roam around everywhere. He received no free drop. He said, "I can hit this shot by just pitching it off with a wedge, no problem." Unfortunately, he hit it fat, and the cow pile went all over him. He smelled terrible, but we laughed about this incident the entire three months we were there.

LEFT TO RIGHT: *Walter Hall, Jerry McGee, Tom Kite, Christy O'Connor, Jr., Andy North*

Some players on the SENIOR TOUR can be very ingenious when it comes to doing their laundry. One of the easiest ways allows you to stay in your room, watch television and get the wash done at the same time. You just fill up the bath tub with water and put in some soap and the clothes. After the clothes have soaked for a while, use a golf club to agitate them. Drain and rinse and spread the clothes around the room to dry.

SPINACH PUFF

Gil Morgan

2 (10-ounce) packages frozen chopped spinach, cooked, drained

8 ounces cream cheese, softened

$1/2$ cup milk

$1/4$ cup ($1/2$ stick) butter, melted

$1/4$ teaspoon nutmeg

salt and pepper to taste

3 eggs, beaten

$1^{1}/2$ cups crushed wheat cracker crumbs

$1/2$ cup shredded Cheddar cheese

Combine the spinach and cream cheese in a bowl and mix well. Add the milk, butter, nutmeg, salt and pepper and mix well. Stir in the eggs. Spoon $1/2$ of the spinach mixture into a greased 9×9-inch baking dish. Sprinkle with $1/2$ of the cracker crumbs. Spoon the remaining spinach mixture over the crumbs and top with the Cheddar cheese. Sprinkle with the remaining cracker crumbs.

Bake at 350 degrees for 30 minutes or until puffed and golden brown.

Serves 6

O N T H E G R E E N • S A L A D S • S I D E D I S H E S

My brother Dave was a Marine during the Vietnam War. While overseas, he would follow my career by reading Stars and Stripes. *I was playing well at the time, but hadn't won in more than a year. Dave was due to return to the states and wrote to ask if he could caddy for me in a few events. He felt that he could guide me to my next victory. The Tour was just about to begin its Florida swing when Dave was discharged, so he drove from California to join me. Although I played and finished well, I didn't win one event. Dave returned home after four weeks on Tour with me, and wouldn't you know that I won the very next week at the Florida Citrus Open.*

ROASTED VEGETABLES

Bob Lunn

1/3 cup white balsamic vinegar	8 ounces baby carrots
2 tablespoons olive oil	1 red bell pepper
1 1/2 teaspoons molasses	1 yellow bell pepper
1 teaspoon Italian seasoning	2 yellow squash
1/4 teaspoon salt	2 zucchini
1/4 teaspoon pepper	1 large onion, chopped
1 bunch green onions, sliced	

Whisk together the balsamic vinegar, olive oil, molasses, Italian seasoning, salt and pepper in a small bowl. Stir in the green onions.

Cut the carrots, red pepper, yellow pepper, yellow squash and zucchini into 1-inch pieces. Toss with the onion in a large bowl. Pour the vinegar mixture over the vegetables and toss to coat.

Let stand for 30 minutes, stirring occasionally. Drain the vegetables, reserving the liquid. Arrange the vegetables in a shallow roasting pan. Roast at 400 degrees for 15 minutes or until tender-crisp, stirring occasionally.

Toss the roasted vegetables with the reserved vinegar mixture. You may serve immediately or chill, covered, for up to 8 hours.

Serves 6

One of the best perks of playing on the SENIOR TOUR is the variety of food everywhere we play. The geographic areas of our country have a wide range of interesting foods. From fried dill pickles to grits, to sushi to bratwurst, we enjoy great new dining experiences. Some of us have also been lucky enough to experience the cuisine of many countries and to know players from other countries. We not only get to taste new and exciting food, but we also learn about the whys and hows involved in the making of some of the delicacies. Sometimes, however, it's best not to know just exactly what you're eating until later. Thanks to all who help expand our palates and waistlines!

BASMATI RICE WITH VEGETABLES

Gary McCord

1 (8-ounce) package basmati rice
2 ounces feta cheese
$^1/_2$ cup asparagus tips, steamed
$^1/_4$ cup chopped oil-pack sun-dried tomatoes
$^1/_4$ cup toasted pine nuts

Cook the rice using the package directions. Combine the cooked rice, feta cheese, asparagus, sun-dried tomatoes and pine nuts in a microwave-safe dish. Microwave, covered, on Low for 3 to 4 minutes or until the cheese melts.

Serves 4 to 6

ON THE GREEN • SALADS • SIDE DISHES

Trust children to tell it like it is. Four-year-old Jackie was on the practice range one day while I was practicing when a man, being nice and friendly, asked him what his daddy did. Jackie replied, "Oh, nothing. He just plays golf."

RICE PILAF

Jack Nicklaus

$1/2$ cup (1 stick) butter
8 ounces mushrooms, sliced
$1/2$ onion, chopped
$3/4$ cup uncooked rice
$3/4$ teaspoon oregano

$3/4$ teaspoon paprika
1 (10-ounce) can beef consommé
$3/4$ cup water
$1/2$ cup sherry

Melt the butter in a large saucepan. Stir in the mushrooms, onion, rice, oregano and paprika. Cook for 20 minutes, stirring occasionally. Add the beef consommé, water and sherry and mix well. Spoon the mixture into a baking dish. Bake, covered, at 400 degrees for 45 minutes. Remove the cover and bake for 15 minutes longer.

Serves 8

This fish, weighing more than 50 pounds, was a record permit catch and release

I am one of the lucky golfers who has enjoyed having a wife or significant other caddy for me on Tour, as it is a special relationship. Others who have enjoyed the same experience include: Hugh Baiocchi, Butch Baird, Jim Dent, Bob Eastwood, Dick Hendrickson, Bunky Henry, Bob Lunn, Tommy McGinnis, Calvin Peete, Gary Player, Jimmy Powell, Rocky Thompson, Steve Veriato, Tom Watson, Bob Wynn and Walter Zembriski.

PASTA WITH BASIL SAUCE

Ed Sneed

Basil sauce is also good on ravioli. Serve the pasta with a tossed green salad and bread for a first course or light supper.

5 large garlic cloves, minced

1/3 cup extra-virgin olive oil

1 (29-ounce) can Italian tomato purée

1 cup packed fresh basil, chopped

salt and pepper to taste

16 ounces angel hair pasta, cooked

Sauté the garlic in the olive oil in a saucepan until tender; do not brown. Stir in the tomato purée and basil. Simmer over medium heat for 15 to 20 minutes, stirring occasionally. Season with the salt and pepper. Serve over the pasta.

Serves 6 to 8

ON THE GREEN • SALADS • SIDE DISHES

Our first five children were born in a six-year period, and our sixth child was born eight years later. Traveling from South Africa to the United States was a challenge in those years! Our wives all wonder how they ever managed without disposable diapers and all of the other great innovations that parents enjoy today. As Barbara Nicklaus says, "We did what we had to do."

RISOTTO FAGIOLI

Gary Player

Be sure not to add too much liquid at one time, or you will drown the risotto, and always use a fork to stir the risotto.

2 garlic cloves, crushed
2 tablespoons olive oil
500 grams uncooked arborio rice
1 liter chicken or vegetable broth
1 (410-gram) can white kidney beans
1/2 bunch parsley, chopped
3 1/2 ounces grated Parmesan cheese
1/8 teaspoon salt
pepper to taste

Sauté the garlic in the olive oil in a heavy saucepan until tender. Add the rice and 1 cup of the broth. Cook until the broth is absorbed, stirring constantly.

Add the remaining broth to the rice, 1 cup at a time, cooking until the broth is absorbed and the rice is tender after each addition, stirring constantly. Stir in the beans, parsley, Parmesan cheese, salt and pepper.

Remove from the heat and let stand, covered with a tight-fitting lid, for 2 to 5 minutes. Serve on heated plates.

Refer to the Metric Conversion Chart on page 215 for measurement equivalents.

Serves 6

One year at the U.S. Open, Jack Nicklaus got on the elevator with us, and our children were so awestruck they couldn't speak. The next day a friend asked them who was the greatest golfer in the world. They, in unison, answered, "Jack Nicklaus." Our friend told them that they should have said that Larry Ziegler was the best golfer, to which they responded, "Well, he's our daddy, and he's the best daddy in the world."

STUFFING CASSEROLE

Larry Ziegler

2 carrots, julienned
2 zucchini, julienned
1 small onion, chopped
1 (10-ounce) can cream of chicken soup
1 cup sour cream
1 (6-ounce) package chicken-flavored stuffing mix
1/2 cup (1 stick) butter, melted

Combine the carrots, zucchini and onion with water to cover in a saucepan. Bring to a boil and boil for 5 minutes; drain. Combine the vegetable mixture with the soup, sour cream and stuffing mix in a bowl and mix well. Spoon into a baking dish. Drizzle with the butter. Bake at 350 degrees for 35 minutes.

Serves 4

ON THE GREEN • SALADS • SIDE DISHES

We were staying in a hotel in Joplin, Missouri, on the way home from a tournament in Fort Worth. We were so tired that we just unpacked my golf clubs and our overnight things and planned an early morning departure. When my wife Joanna got up at 5:30 to exercise, she opened the drapes and saw a black funnel cloud in the distance. We dressed and rushed to the hotel lobby as the tornado went right over the hotel. The noise—and damage—was unbelievable. The hotel was without electricity or water, and our car was totally demolished. Joanna calmed the kids and got our possessions back together, while I hitched a ride to the airport to rent a car. We loaded up and headed home. Needless to say the kids were frightened of storms after that, so I calmed them by telling them that the noise was just a tater wagon rolling around in heaven and some of the taters were falling off.

EGGS FLORENTINE

Larry Ziegler

1/2 cup shredded aged Cheddar cheese

1 (10-ounce) package frozen spinach, thawed, drained

2 slices white bread, crusts trimmed, cubed

1 cup sliced mushrooms

1/2 cup chopped green onions

1 ounce sliced pimento or red bell pepper

6 eggs

1 cup half-and-half

1/2 cup water

salt and pepper to taste

1/2 cup shredded aged Cheddar cheese

1/2 teaspoon paprika

Layer 1/2 cup Cheddar cheese, spinach, bread, mushrooms, green onions and pimento in a greased slow cooker. Combine the eggs, half-and-half, water, salt and pepper in a bowl and beat until blended. Pour over the layers. Sprinkle with 1/2 cup Cheddar cheese and paprika. Cook on Medium for 1 1/2 hours.

Serves 4

GARLIC CHEESE GRITS

....

Larry Mowry

We love this dish in the South, especially with holiday meals.

4 cups water

1 teaspoon salt

2 garlic cloves, pressed

1 cup uncooked grits

3 cups shredded sharp Cheddar cheese

$^1/_2$ cup (1 stick) butter

1 teaspoon seasoned pepper

1 teaspoon Worcestershire sauce

$^1/_4$ teaspoon hot sauce

3 eggs, beaten

paprika

Bring the water, salt and garlic to a boil in a large saucepan. Stir in the grits gradually. Bring to a boil. Reduce the heat and cook for 15 minutes or until thickened, stirring occasionally.

Add the Cheddar cheese, butter, pepper, Worcestershire sauce and hot sauce and mix well. Cook until the cheese melts, stirring occasionally. Remove from the heat and let stand for 10 minutes. Stir in the eggs.

Pour the mixture into a lightly greased 7×11-inch baking dish. Sprinkle with paprika. Bake at 350 degrees for 1 hour or until set.

Serves 8 to 10

ON THE GREEN • SALADS • SIDE DISHES

PINEAPPLE CASSEROLE

Larry Nelson

2 (20-ounce) cans pineapple chunks
1 (20-ounce) can crushed pineapple
2/3 cup sugar
5 teaspoons flour

2 cups shredded sharp Cheddar cheese
1 sleeve butter crackers, crushed
1/4 cup (1/2 stick) butter, melted

Drain the pineapple, reserving 1/2 cup of the juice. Spread the pineapple in a 2-quart baking dish sprayed with nonstick cooking spray.

Combine the sugar, flour and reserved pineapple juice in a bowl and mix well. Pour over the pineapple. Sprinkle with the Cheddar cheese and cracker crumbs. Drizzle with the butter. Bake at 350 degrees for 30 minutes. Serve with ham or other pork dishes.

Serves 10

Drew and Josh Nelson

THE

19TH HOLE

· DESSERTS ·

BANANAS FOSTER

. . . .

Jim Albus

This has always been my favorite restaurant dessert. I now like to make it for dinner parties at home. Be sure to have a lid ready, if necessary, to help put out the flame, and keep the rum bottle away from the flame.

4 bananas
2 cups packed dark brown sugar
1 cup (2 sticks) butter or margarine
2 teaspoons cinnamon
1 cup banana liqueur
1/2 cup (100+ proof) rum
8 scoops vanilla ice cream

Cut each banana into halves. Cut each half lengthwise into quarters; set aside. Combine the brown sugar, butter and cinnamon in a skillet. Cook over low heat until the butter is melted and the mixture is blended, stirring constantly.

Add the banana liqueur and bananas and cook until the bananas are slightly brown, stirring frequently. Pour the rum in slowly and cook for 10 seconds, stirring constantly. Tilt the pan or use a match to ignite. When the flames subside, serve over ice cream.

Serves 8

THE 19TH HOLE • DESSERTS

My wife was caddying for me in a qualifying tournament when one of the other players "whiffed" on a shot. She asked Dana Quigley if that was a "fresh air." When Dana didn't understand, she explained that in South Africa a whiff is called a "fresh air." This sent Dana to the ground with laughter. Some other expressions of that sort that the players have learned from each other include: takkies for sneakers; jumper for sweater; runner for chip shot; level for even par; didn't pitch up for didn't show up; brolly for umbrella; bubbler for drinking fountain; cheeky for cocky; and loo for bathroom.

QUICK BANANA DESSERT

Hugh Baiocchi

This dessert is better when it is made the day before and kept covered in the refrigerator.

4 large ripe bananas
1/3 cup lemon juice
1 1/2 cups chopped pecans
16 ounces light whipped topping
whole pecans

Mash the bananas in a bowl. Stir in the lemon juice. Fold in the chopped pecans and whipped topping. Spoon into a glass serving dish. Top with the whole pecans. Chill, covered, until ready to serve.

Serves 8

I was eagerly awaiting the arrival of Valerie while playing a tournament in Crans-Sur-Sierre in Switzerland in 1984 and had gotten a special room with a balcony and a spectacular view of the Alps. Earlier in the day I had gone shopping at the local market and purchased Champagne, Beluga caviar, eggs and toast points. I was very proud of myself, as shopping with my limited French vocabulary was no easy matter. The spread looked great, but Valerie was suspicious when the eggs were still in the shell. I assured her that I had ordered hard-boiled eggs, but she wasn't convinced, so I took the eggs to the balcony to peel them. When I cracked them, raw egg went everywhere. I turned and saw Val nodding her head with that knowing smile on her face.

CHOCOLATE MOUSSE WITH BRANDY

John Jacobs

8 ounces dark chocolate

4 eggs, separated

1 teaspoon brandy

Melt the chocolate in a double boiler over simmering water; remove from the heat. Pour the chocolate into a mixing bowl. Beat in the egg yolks until blended. Stir in the brandy. Beat the egg whites until stiff peaks form. Fold the egg whites into the chocolate mixture.

Spoon the mixture gently into a large serving bowl or 4 individual serving bowls. Chill, covered, for 3 hours before serving.

Serves 4

THE 19TH HOLE • DESSERTS

CHOCOLATE CHEESECAKE

Tom Kite

GRAHAM CRACKER CRUST
1^{1}/4 cups graham cracker crumbs
^{1}/4 cup (^{1}/2 stick) margarine, melted
2 tablespoons sugar

FILLING
^{1}/2 cup semisweet chocolate chips
^{1}/4 cup sugar
16 ounces cream cheese, softened
^{3}/4 cup sugar
^{1}/2 cup sour cream
1 teaspoon vanilla extract
4 eggs

For the crust, combine the graham cracker crumbs, margarine and sugar in a bowl and mix well. Press over the bottom and 1^{1}/2 inches up the side of a 9-inch springform pan.

For the filling, combine the chocolate chips and ^{1}/4 cup sugar in a double boiler over hot, but not boiling, water and heat until blended, stirring frequently; remove from the heat.

Beat the cream cheese in a mixing bowl until light and fluffy. Beat in ^{3}/4 cup sugar. Add the sour cream and vanilla and mix well. Beat in the eggs 1 at a time. Divide the mixture in half.

Stir the chocolate mixture into one half of the cream cheese mixture. Spoon into the prepared pan. Spoon the remaining cream cheese mixture over the top. Cut through the layers with a knife to marbleize.

Bake at 325 degrees for 40 to 50 minutes or until the center is almost set when gently shaken. Cool on a wire rack and chill, covered, until ready to serve.

Serves 10

MOTHER'S ITALIAN CHEESECAKE

Jerry Heard

16 ounces cream cheese, softened
2 cups ricotta cheese
1 1/2 cups sugar
4 eggs, at room temperature
1/4 cup (1/2 stick) unsalted butter, melted, cooled
3 tablespoons cornstarch
3 tablespoons flour
2 1/2 teaspoons vanilla extract
2 cups sour cream

Beat the cream cheese, ricotta cheese and sugar in a mixing bowl until blended. Beat in the eggs 1 at a time. Add the butter, cornstarch, flour and vanilla and mix well. Fold in the sour cream. Spoon into a 9-inch springform pan.

Bake at 325 degrees for 1 hour. Turn off the oven and let stand in oven for 2 hours. Cool on a wire rack and chill, covered, for 1 1/2 hours or longer.

Serves 10

THE 19TH HOLE • DESSERTS

Some players are more verbose than others in their disagreements with the Tour officials. One day one of those players, who was trying to keep his words in check, asked for a ruling. He didn't get the ruling that he thought was correct. Remembering that he didn't want to get fined for saying the wrong thing, he asked the Tour official if he could be fined for what he was thinking. When the Tour official replied, "No," the player said, "Well then, I think you're an A—!"

DA' BOMB

. . . .

Billy Casper

This is easy to make, beautiful to look at and yummy to taste.

1 (2-layer) package chocolate cake mix
2 (4-ounce) packages chocolate instant pudding mix
1 (16-ounce) container whipped topping
6 Skor candy bars, chopped

Prepare and bake the cake mix using the package directions. Cool to room temperature. Prepare the pudding mixes using the package directions. Break the cake into bite-size pieces.

Layer the cake pieces, pudding, whipped topping and candy bar pieces $1/3$ at a time in a large glass bowl. Chill, covered, until ready to serve.

Serves 12

Winnie Palmer always traveled with a jar of instant spiced tea mix for a quick pick up. To enjoy her special recipe, just mix 1/2 cup instant tea granules with 2 1/2 cups sugar, 2 cups of instant orange drink mix and two 3-ounce packages of lemonade mix. Add 2 teaspoons each ground cloves and cinnamon, mix well and store in an airtight container. Add 2 or 3 teaspoons of the mix to a cup of boiling water and stir to mix well.

FRUIT CITRINE

Arnold Palmer

1 (16-ounce) can sliced apples

1/2 cup grated coconut

6 maraschino cherries, finely chopped

6 minted cherries, finely chopped

1 center lemon slice with rind, finely chopped

1 center orange slice with rind, finely chopped

1/2 cup sugar

1 teaspoon vanilla extract

1/2 teaspoon cinnamon

1/2 teaspoon nutmeg

1 teaspoon yellow food coloring

1/3 stick butter

cornstarch (optional)

Combine the apples, coconut, cherries, lemon rind and orange rind in a saucepan and mix well. Stir in the sugar, vanilla, cinnamon, nutmeg, food coloring and butter. Bring to a boil, stirring to mix well.

Blend cornstarch with a small amount of water and add to the mixture if needed for the desired consistency. Cook until thickened, stirring constantly.

Serves 4

THE 19TH HOLE • DESSERTS

CREME BRULEE

Graham Marsh

3 eggs
$^1/_4$ cup sugar
$^1/_4$ teaspoon salt
2 cups heavy cream
brown sugar

Combine the eggs, sugar and salt in a bowl and mix well. Heat the heavy cream in a saucepan just until warm. Stir into the egg mixture. Transfer the mixture to the top of a double boiler and cook over simmering water until it lightly coats the back of a metal spoon, stirring constantly. Cook for 2 minutes longer, stirring constantly. Pour the mixture into 4 ramekins. Chill, covered, until ready to serve. Sprinkle the top of each ramekin with brown sugar. Place the ramekins in a large baking dish. Add equal amounts of water and ice cubes to the baking dish. Broil just until the brown sugar is melted.

Serves 4

LEFT TO RIGHT: *Andy North, Graham Marsh, Lanny Wadkins*

As they were playing a round, Chi Chi said to Lee Trevino, "Please entertain the crowd while I go to the porta-potty." Just as Chi Chi arrived at his destination, Trevino called, "Mention my name, you can get a good seat." Not to be outdone, Chi Chi called back, "Take it to Tijuana and rent it out as a condo." Lee replied, "You couldn't rent out the top floor."

GELATIN ICE CREAM

Chi Chi Rodriguez

1 teaspoon mayonnaise
2 (3-ounce) packages orange gelatin
1 (3-ounce) package lemon gelatin
2^1/$_2$ cups warm water
^{1}/$_2$ cup sugar
1 envelope unflavored gelatin
^{1}/$_2$ cup water
1 pint vanilla ice cream, softened

Grease a 9x9-inch pan with the mayonnaise. Combine the orange gelatin, lemon gelatin, 2^1/$_2$ cups water and sugar in a bowl and mix well. Dissolve the unflavored gelatin in ^{1}/$_2$ cup water.

Pour the unflavored gelatin mixture into the orange gelatin mixture and mix well. Add the ice cream and stir until blended. Spoon the mixture into the prepared pan. Chill, covered, until set.

Serves 8

THE 19TH HOLE • DESSERTS

PANACHE TRUFFLE DESSERT

Jay Sigel

8 ounces semisweet chocolate
1 cup sugar
1 cup (2 sticks) unsalted butter
1/2 cup brewed coffee
4 eggs
1 cup whipping cream
1/4 cup confectioners' sugar
1/4 teaspoon vanilla extract
strawberries or raspberries (optional)

Cover the bottom of an 8¹/2-inch springform pan with foil. Butter the bottom and side of the pan. Combine the chocolate, sugar and butter in a microwave-safe bowl. Microwave just until the chocolate and butter melt. Stir to mix well. Cool to room temperature. Stir in the coffee. Beat in the eggs.

Pour the mixture into the prepared pan. Bake at 350 degrees for 30 minutes or until a crust forms. Cool to room temperature. Chill, covered, for 8 hours. Remove the side of the pan.

Beat the whipping cream, confectioners' sugar and vanilla in a mixing bowl until stiff peaks form. Spoon the whipped cream over the top of the dessert. Top with strawberries or raspberries.

You may prepare the dessert up to 5 days in advance. Keep chilled in the refrigerator and top with whipped cream just before serving.

Serves 8

STICKY TOFFEE PUDDING

Dale Douglass

Scotland is the original home of this delicious dessert as well as to wonderful golf courses and castles.

PUDDING

2 1/2 cups chopped dates

2 teaspoons baking soda

1 cup (2 sticks) butter, softened

1/2 cup sugar

4 eggs

2 1/2 cups flour

2 teaspoons salt

1 tablespoon vanilla extract

1 tablespoon (heaping) baking powder

BUTTERSCOTCH TOPPING

1 cup light corn syrup

1 cup packed brown sugar

1/2 cup milk

3 tablespoons butter

1/2 teaspoon salt

For the pudding, combine the dates with water to cover in a saucepan and bring to a boil. Reduce the heat and simmer for 3 minutes. Stir in the baking soda. Remove from the heat and cool to room temperature. Drain, reserving the dates and 1 cup of the liquid.

Cream the butter and sugar together in a mixing bowl until light and fluffy. Beat in the eggs 1 at a time. Add the flour, salt and vanilla and mix well. Stir in the baking powder and reserved liquid. Add the dates and mix gently.

Spoon the mixture into a buttered 8x8-inch baking pan. Bake at 350 degrees for 30 to 40 minutes or until the top is golden brown.

For the topping, combine the corn syrup, brown sugar, milk, butter and salt in a small saucepan. Cook just until the butter and brown sugar melt, stirring to mix well.

To serve, cut the pudding into servings and place in microwave-safe serving bowls. Spoon the Butterscotch Topping over the servings. Microwave for 30 to 60 seconds or until "sticky." Serve with vanilla ice cream.

You may substitute a jar of butterscotch topping for the topping in the recipe if preferred.

Serves 8

My wife and I have enjoyed going to the British Senior Open several times and have stayed for an extra week at Loch Lomond in Scotland to search for Douglas Castles. I discovered Sticky Toffee Pudding for dessert and thought it was wonderful! The waitress secured the recipe for me, but it was for 40 people and had no instructions. Joyce has cut it down and combined it with a recipe for date pudding and thinks it comes pretty close to the real thing, although we still prefer the pudding at Loch Lomond!

Dale and Joyce Douglass

THE BEST TIRAMISU

Jerry Heard

6 egg yolks

1 cup sugar

2 tablespoons Marsala or coffee liqueur

16 ounces mascarpone cheese

6 egg whites

1 package ladyfingers

1 cup strong coffee

baking cocoa

Beat the egg yolks and sugar in a mixing bowl until blended. Add the wine and mascarpone cheese and beat until light and fluffy.

Beat the egg whites in a bowl until stiff peaks form. Fold the beaten egg whites into the cheese mixture.

Dip the ladyfingers in the coffee. Layer half the ladyfingers, cheese mixture and remaining ladyfingers in a shallow 3-quart serving dish. Sprinkle with baking cocoa. Chill, covered, for 8 hours or longer.

Serves 10

THE 19TH HOLE • DESSERTS

As Susan and I were driving to Miami, Susan entertained our three-year-old daughter with stories about where we were going and what fun we would have there. When I announced that we were almost to Miami, my daughter reprimanded me, saying that it was not my "ami," it was Mommy's "ami."

BROWNIE TRIFLE

Andy North

2 packages extra-moist brownie mix
2 (6-ounce) packages chocolate instant pudding mix
6 cups milk
18 to 24 ounces whipped topping
6 Skor candy bars, crushed

Prepare the brownie mixes using the package directions. Cool to room temperature. Break into bite-size pieces. Prepare the pudding mixes using the 6 cups of milk. Do not chill the pudding.

Layer the brownie pieces, pudding, whipped topping and crushed candy bars 1/3 at a time in a 3-quart trifle bowl. Chill, covered, for 8 hours or longer.

You may decorate the trifle with chocolate curls or leaves if desired.

Serves 12

SHERRY TRIFLE

John Morgan

4 small sponge cakes
2 to 3 tablespoons your favorite jam
4 to 5 tablespoons sweet sherry
3 tablespoons water
1 tablespoon sugar
2 cups prepared custard
blanched almonds to taste
$1/2$ cup heavy cream
glacé cherries
angelica
chopped mixed nuts

Slice each sponge cake horizontally into halves. Spread one side of each sponge cake with the jam. Arrange the sponge cakes in a serving dish.

Combine the sherry, water and sugar in a saucepan. Cook until the sugar is dissolved, stirring frequently. Pour over the sponge cakes to moisten. Pour the custard over the prepared sponge cakes. Sprinkle with the almonds. Chill, covered with a plate, for 2 to 3 hours. Trifle may be frozen for 1 to 2 weeks before serving.

To serve, pour the heavy cream over the chilled trifle. Garnish with the cherries and angelica. Sprinkle with the nuts.

You may use sweet white wine in place of the sherry and water if desired.

Serves 6

My 15-year-old grandson Jimmy caddied for me one summer and was there for the NFL Classic when Cadillac introduced the Escalade SUV, offering it as part of the prize package for the winner of the tournament. Jimmy admired the vehicle every day and finally I told him that if I won, I would give it to him for his 16th birthday.

I was in a play-off for the win on Sunday, and the ESPN cameras focused on Jimmy biting a towel as he watched "Coach" putt. The announcers kept commenting on how hard Jimmy was pulling for his grandfather, not realizing that Jimmy was most interested in who was going to get that car! I lost the play-off, but the shots of Jimmy appeared on ESPN for two days.

MICROWAVE PEANUT BRITTLE

Jim Colbert

The times for this recipe are based on an 800-watt microwave.

1 cup raw peanuts

1 cup sugar

$1/2$ cup light corn syrup

$1/4$ teaspoon salt

1 teaspoon butter

1 teaspoon vanilla extract

1 teaspoon baking soda

Combine the peanuts, sugar, corn syrup and salt in a 2-quart microwave-safe dish and mix well with a wooden spoon. Microwave on High for 4 minutes leaving the wooden spoon in the dish. Stir the mixture and microwave on High for 3 minutes longer.

Stir in the butter and vanilla. Microwave on High for $1^1/2$ minutes. Add the baking soda, stirring quickly.

Pour into a buttered baking sheet, spreading into a thin layer with hands. Let cool completely and break into pieces.

You may wear heavy rubber gloves coated with nonstick cooking spray to spread the brittle if desired.

Serves 20

Some people work out very hard on the Tour to stay in shape. Some realize that they haven't done a very good job staying in shape—the cookies are wonderful! For some, the best way to stay in shape is to put up your feet and enjoy a glass of Belvedere and a cigar.

BUCKEYE BALLS

Larry Mowry

1 (16-ounce) jar creamy peanut butter
1 cup (2 sticks) butter or margarine, softened
1¹/2 (1-pound) packages confectioners' sugar
2 cups semisweet chocolate chips
2 tablespoons shortening

Beat the peanut butter and butter in a mixing bowl until blended. Beat in the confectioners' sugar gradually. Shape into 1-inch balls. Chill for 10 minutes or until firm.

Combine the chocolate chips and shortening in a 2-quart microwave-safe dish. Microwave on High for 1¹/2 minutes or until the chips melt, stirring twice.

Dip the balls into the chocolate mixture using wooden picks and place on waxed paper. Let stand until cool and firm.

Makes 7 dozen

THE 19TH HOLE • DESSERTS

Chocolate Cake

Hale Irwin

This is our favorite birthday cake. We like to serve it with vanilla ice cream and chocolate sauce. It also freezes well and can be reheated in the microwave.

Cake	Chocolate Frosting
2 cups flour	$^1/_2$ cup (1 stick) margarine
2 cups sugar	$^1/_4$ cup baking cocoa
1 teaspoon baking soda	6 tablespoons sour cream
1 teaspoon salt	1 (1-pound) package confectioners' sugar
1 cup (2 sticks) margarine	1 teaspoon vanilla extract
1 cup water	
$^1/_4$ cup baking cocoa	
2 eggs	
$^1/_2$ cup sour cream	
1 teaspoon vanilla extract	

For the cake, sift the flour, sugar, baking soda and salt into a bowl. Combine the margarine and water in a small saucepan. Bring to a boil, stirring frequently. Remove from the heat and stir in the cocoa. Pour the cocoa mixture over the dry ingredients. Beat in the eggs, sour cream and vanilla.

Pour into a greased 10×15-inch baking pan. Bake at 350 degrees for 20 minutes or until the cake tests done.

For the frosting, combine the margarine, cocoa and sour cream in a small saucepan. Bring to a boil, stirring frequently. Remove from the heat and stir in the confectioners' sugar and vanilla. Spread over the warm cake.

Serves 12 to 15

Bob Gilder says that Green Slime packed with Daddy's golf clubs is not a good idea!

FROZEN COCONUT CAKE

Bob Gilder

This recipe was given to the PGA TOUR wives by Louise Nelson.

1 (2-layer) package yellow cake mix
2 (6-ounce) packages frozen shredded coconut
1 cup sour cream
1 cup sugar
8 ounces whipped topping

Prepare and bake the cake in four 9-inch cake pans using the package directions. Cool in the pans for 10 minutes. Remove to a wire rack to cool completely.

Reserve 1 cup of the coconut. Combine the remaining coconut, sour cream and sugar in a bowl and mix well. Reserve 1 cup of the coconut mixture. Spread the remaining coconut mixture between the layers.

Combine the reserved coconut mixture and whipped topping in a bowl and mix well. Spread over the top of the cake. Sprinkle with the reserved coconut. Chill, covered, for 3 days before serving.

You may also freeze the cake, removing it from the freezer 24 hours before serving.

Serves 15 to 20

THE 19TH HOLE • DESSERTS

LEMON CAKE

Bruno Henning

CAKE
2 3/4 cups flour
2 teaspoons baking powder
1/4 teaspoon salt
1 cup (2 sticks) butter or margarine, softened
2 cups sugar
4 eggs
1 cup milk
2 tablespoons (scant) lemon zest

LEMON GLAZE
3/4 cup sugar
1/3 cup lemon juice

For the cake, combine the flour, baking powder and salt in a bowl and mix well. Cream the butter and sugar in a mixing bowl until light and fluffy. Beat in the eggs 1 at a time. Add the dry ingredients alternately with the milk, beginning and ending with the dry ingredients and mixing well after each addition. Stir in the lemon zest.

Spoon into a buttered and floured tube or bundt pan. Bake at 350 degrees for 70 minutes. Cool in the pan for 5 minutes. Invert onto a wire rack.

For the glaze, combine the sugar and lemon juice in a bowl and mix well. Drizzle the glaze over the warm cake.

Serves 16

MAYONNAISE CAKE

. . . .

Hubert Green

CAKE
4 cups flour

4 teaspoons baking soda

2 cups sugar

1/2 cup baking cocoa

2 cups mayonnaise-type salad dressing

2 cups water

2 teaspoons vanilla extract

MOCHA FROSTING
4 cups confectioners' sugar

1/2 cup (1 stick) butter, softened

1/4 cup baking cocoa

2 teaspoons vanilla extract

2/3 teaspoon salt

cold coffee

For the cake, sift the flour and baking soda together. Combine the sugar and cocoa in a large mixing bowl and mix well. Stir in the flour mixture. Add the mayonnaise, water and vanilla gradually, beating until blended.

Spoon into a greased 9×13-inch baking pan. Bake at 350 degrees for 35 to 45 minutes or until a wooden pick inserted near the center comes out clean. Let stand until cool.

For the frosting, sift the confectioners' sugar into a bowl. Add the butter, cocoa, vanilla and salt and mix well. Stir in the coffee 1 teaspoon at a time until of the desired consistency. Spread over the top of the cooled cake.

Serves 15

THE 19TH HOLE • DESSERTS

Jack was on an elevator one time when a lady noticed him and asked, "Do you know who you are?"

OATMEAL CAKE

·····································

Jack Nicklaus

CAKE	BROWN SUGAR COCONUT GLAZE
1 1/2 cups boiling water	1/2 cup (1 stick) butter
1 cup quick-cooking oats	1 cup packed light brown sugar
1 cup sugar	1/2 cup milk
1 cup packed light brown sugar	1 teaspoon vanilla extract
1/2 cup vegetable oil	1 (3 1/2 ounce) can shredded coconut
2 eggs	
1 1/2 cups flour	
1 teaspoon baking soda	
1 teaspoon cinnamon	
1/2 teaspoon salt	

For the cake, pour the boiling water over the oats in a bowl and let stand for several minutes. Combine the sugar, brown sugar and oil in a mixing bowl and beat until smooth. Beat in the eggs 1 at a time.

Mix the flour, baking soda, cinnamon and salt together. Add to the sugar mixture and mix well. Stir in the oats.

Spoon into a greased 9×13-inch cake pan. Bake at 350 degrees for 35 minutes.

For the glaze, melt the butter in a saucepan over medium heat. Add the brown sugar and milk and mix well. Cook to 235 degrees on a candy thermometer, soft-ball stage, stirring constantly. Remove from the heat and stir in the vanilla and coconut.

Pierce the top of the cake with a fork. Pour the glaze over the warm cake.

Serves 15

BROWN SUGAR POUND CAKE

Jack Nicklaus

CAKE

1 cup (2 sticks) butter, softened
1/2 cup shortening
1 (1-pound) package light brown sugar
1 cup sugar
5 eggs
3 cups sifted flour
1 teaspoon baking powder
1/2 teaspoon salt
1 cup milk
1 teaspoon vanilla extract
1 cup chopped pecans (optional)

BROWN SUGAR PECAN GLAZE

1/2 cup packed light brown sugar
2 tablespoons butter
2 tablespoons shortening
2 tablespoons milk
1/2 teaspoon salt
1 teaspoon vanilla extract
1/2 cup ground pecans

For the cake, cream the butter and shortening in a mixing bowl until light. Add the brown sugar and sugar and beat until fluffy. Beat in the eggs 1 at a time.

Sift the flour, baking powder and salt together. Add to the creamed mixture alternately with the milk and vanilla, mixing well after each addition. Stir in the pecans.

Spoon the mixture into a greased bundt pan. Bake at 350 degrees for 1 1/4 hours. Cool in the pan for 5 minutes. Invert onto a baking pan.

For the glaze, combine the brown sugar, butter, shortening, milk and salt in a saucepan. Bring to a boil, stirring constantly; remove from the heat. Stir in the vanilla and pecans. Drizzle the glaze over the cake. Broil until the glaze is bubbly.

Serves 16

Barbara was trying to make the evening special for our youngest son's future in-laws, so she made a birthday cake for his future father-in-law and hid it in the oven. She forgot it, however, and when she turned on the oven later in the day to cook the Veal Parmesan, the frosting had melted and run down the cake before she rescued it. We ate it anyway and laughed at the story, which broke the ice and is still a great conversation piece with our son's in-laws.

RED VELVET CAKE

Jack Nicklaus

CAKE	CREAM CHEESE FROSTING
1½ cups sugar	½ cup (1 stick) butter, softened
1½ cups vegetable oil	1 (1-pound) package confectioners' sugar
1 cup buttermilk	8 ounces cream cheese, softened
2 eggs	1 teaspoon vanilla extract
1 tablespoon vanilla extract	1 cup chopped pecans (optional)
½ bottle red food coloring	
2½ cups flour	
1 tablespoon baking cocoa	
1 tablespoon baking soda	

For the cake, combine the sugar, oil, buttermilk, eggs, vanilla and food coloring in a mixing bowl and beat until blended. Sift the flour, baking cocoa and baking soda together. Add to the buttermilk mixture and mix well.

Pour into 3 greased and floured 9-inch round cake pans. Bake at 350 degrees for 15 to 20 minutes or until cakes test done. Cool in the pans for 10 minutes. Remove to a wire rack to cool completely.

For the frosting, combine the butter, confectioners' sugar, cream cheese, vanilla and pecans in a bowl and mix well. Spread between the layers and over the top and side of the cooled cake.

Serves 12

Joe Inman's pen once leaked in his back pocket, leaving a black spot. He just took the pen out and drew a smiley face on his bottom for everyone to see as he lined up his putts.

CREME DE MENTHE BROWNIES

Joe Inman, Jr.

BROWNIES	FILLING AND TOPPING
4 ounces unsweetened chocolate	1/4 cup crème de menthe
1 cup (2 sticks) butter	green food coloring
4 eggs	1/2 cup (1 stick) butter, softened
2 cups sugar	1 (1-pound) package confectioners' sugar
1 teaspoon vanilla extract	8 ounces semisweet chocolate chips
1 cup flour	1/4 cup (1/2 stick) butter
1/2 teaspoon salt	3 tablespoons water

For the brownies, place the chocolate in a microwave-safe dish. Microwave for 1 minute. Add the butter and microwave until melted, stirring at 1-minute intervals. Cool to room temperature.

Beat the eggs in a large mixing bowl until thick and pale yellow. Beat the sugar in gradually. Add the vanilla, flour, salt and chocolate mixture and beat for 1 minute longer.

Pour into a greased 9x13-inch baking dish. Bake at 325 degrees for 25 minutes. Brownies will be "fudgy." Cool to room temperature.

For the filling and topping, tint the crème de menthe with a few drops of the green food coloring. Combine the crème de menthe, 1/2 cup butter and 1/2 of the confectioners' sugar in a bowl and mix well. Stir in enough additional confectioners' sugar to make a creamy consistency. Spread over the brownies.

Combine the chocolate chips and 1/4 cup butter in a microwave-safe dish. Microwave until melted. Add the water and stir until blended. Spread over the filling. Chill, covered, until ready to serve. Let stand until room temperature before cutting to serve.

For a variation, you may substitute raspberry liqueur and red food coloring or orange liqueur and orange food coloring for the crème de menthe and green food coloring.

Serves 20 to 30

THE 19TH HOLE • DESSERTS

One day I rushed down and put our week's laundry in the front seat of the white Cadillac courtesy car provided for each golfer. When I realized that I had forgotten something, I shut and locked the car and dashed back to the room. I came back to discover that I had locked my laundry in someone else's white Cadillac!

FAVORITE CHOCOLATE CHIP COOKIES

Dick Lotz

Our daughter Nina used to bake these cookies and next-day air them to us on the Tour when I would have a top ten finish. The ESPN crew became quite fond of these home-baked goodies.

2 cups (4 sticks) butter, softened
2 cups packed brown sugar
1 1/2 cups sugar
4 eggs
2 teaspoons vanilla extract
5 cups rolled oats
4 cups flour
2 teaspoons baking powder
2 teaspoons baking soda
1 teaspoon salt
4 cups semisweet chocolate chips

Cream the butter, brown sugar and sugar in a mixing bowl until light and fluffy. Beat in the eggs and vanilla.

Process the oats in a blender until finely ground. Combine the oats, flour, baking powder, baking soda and salt together. Add to the creamed mixture gradually, mixing well after each addition. Stir in the chocolate chips.

Drop by teaspoonfuls 2 inches apart onto a nonstick cookie sheet. Bake at 375 degrees for 10 minutes. Cool on the cookie sheet for several minutes. Remove to a wire rack to cool completely.

Makes 8 to 9 dozen

Ed Dougherty made a pact with God during the Vietnam War. He was in a foxhole during a violent shelling when he promised God that he would never miss Mass on Sunday if he survived that battle. Ed was one of the lucky ones to make it through that night, and he has never missed Mass at home or while traveling on the Tour since then.

ULTIMATE CHOCOLATE CHIP COOKIES

Ed Dougherty

1 cup walnuts

5 tablespoons butter, softened

5 tablespoons shortening

3/4 cup packed brown sugar

1 egg

2 tablespoons honey

1 1/2 teaspoons vanilla extract

1 1/2 cups flour

1 teaspoon baking powder

1/2 teaspoon baking soda

1 1/2 cups semisweet chocolate chips

Arrange the walnuts on a baking sheet. Bake at 325 degrees for 10 minutes or until light brown, stirring frequently. Cool to room temperature and chop the walnuts.

Cream the butter, shortening and brown sugar in a mixing bowl until light and fluffy. Beat in the egg. Stir in the honey and vanilla. Mix the flour, baking powder and baking soda together. Add to the creamed mixture gradually, beating well after each addition. Stir in the walnuts and chocolate chips.

Drop by teaspoonfuls 2 inches apart onto a lightly greased cookie sheet. Bake at 375 degrees for 8 to 9 minutes or until light brown. Cool on the cookie sheet for several minutes. Remove to a wire rack to cool completely.

Makes 4 dozen

THE 19TH HOLE • DESSERTS

POTATO CHIP COOKIES

Bob Murphy

1 cup (2 sticks) butter or margarine, softened
1/2 cup sugar
1 teaspoon vanilla extract

1 cup crushed potato chips
1 cup flour
sugar

Cream the butter, 1/2 cup sugar and vanilla in a mixing bowl until light and fluffy. Add the crushed potato chips and mix well. Stir in the flour. Shape into balls. Place 2 inches apart on an ungreased cookie sheet. Flatten with a glass dipped in additional sugar. Bake at 350 degrees for 16 to 18 minutes or until light brown. Cool on the cookie sheet for several minutes. Remove to a wire rack to cool completely.

Make 2 to 3 dozen

When I hit my ball into a water hazard, I looked it over and decided to hit it. I took off my shoe and sock, rolled up my pants leg, took a stance and hit the ball. Only then did I realize that I had taken off the wrong shoe and sock.

FROSTED ITALIAN COOKIES

Mike McCullough

COOKIES
$1/2$ cup shortening

1 cup sugar

8 eggs

1 teaspoon vanilla extract

3 cups (or more) flour

1 tablespoon baking powder

VANILLA FROSTING
2 cups confectioners' sugar

$1/4$ cup ($1/2$ stick) butter, softened

1 teaspoon vanilla extract

For the cookies, combine the shortening, sugar, eggs and vanilla in a mixing bowl and beat until blended. Combine the flour and baking powder in a bowl. Add to the egg mixture and mix until smooth, adding additional flour as needed.

Drop by teaspoonfuls 2 inches apart onto an ungreased cookie sheet. Bake at 350 degrees for 10 minutes. Cool on the cookie sheet for several minutes. Remove to a wire rack to cool completely.

For the frosting, combine the confectioners' sugar, butter and vanilla in a bowl and mix well. Spread over the cookies. You may add a drop of food coloring if desired.

Makes 3 dozen

THE 19TH HOLE • DESSERTS

CHOCOLATE CHESS PIE

....

Leonard Thompson

1/2 cup (1 stick) butter

1 ounce chocolate

2 eggs, beaten

1 cup sugar

1 teaspoon vanilla extract

1 unbaked pie shell

Melt the butter in a saucepan over low heat, stirring frequently. Remove from the heat and stir in the chocolate until melted. Cool to room temperature. Stir in the eggs, sugar and vanilla. Pour into the pie shell. Bake at 350 degrees for 30 minutes.

You may substitute a mixture of 3 tablespoons of baking cocoa and 1 tablespoon of vegetable oil for the chocolate if desired.

Serves 6 to 8

SUGAR-FREE APPLE PIE

Walter Morgan

4 red Delicious apples
4 Golden Delicious apples
$^{1}/_{2}$ cup Equal
1 tablespoon flour
1 teaspoon cinnamon
1 teaspoon nutmeg
$^{1}/_{2}$ teaspoon allspice
1 recipe (2-crust) pie pastry
$^{1}/_{2}$ tablespoon butter

Peel, core and slice the apples and place in salted water to cover. Drain the water and rinse the apples. Combine the Equal, flour, cinnamon, nutmeg and allspice in a bowl and mix well. Add the apples, tossing gently to coat.

Spoon the apple mixture into a pastry-lined 9-inch pie plate. Dot with the butter. Top with the remaining pastry, sealing the edge and cutting vents. Cover the edge of the pie with strips of aluminum foil. Bake at 400 degrees for 1 hour or until bubbly. Cover loosely with aluminum foil if necessary to prevent overbrowning.

Serves 8

THE 19TH HOLE • DESSERTS

A golfer brought a friend to caddie at the British Open one year. On the third hole, he made a birdie at the same time that his caddie had eaten part of a large toffee bar. On the fourth hole the caddie ate another part of the toffee bar, and the golfer got another birdie. Same on the fifth, sixth, seventh and eighth holes. That toffee was playing great! The caddie finished the toffee bar, and the golfer sent his son to get him another. As the golfer stood over the ball on the ninth hole, he heard a wrapper being opened. He backed away and looked at his caddie; the caddie stopped. He got ready to hit the ball again, and again came the crackling sound. He backed away again, and, seeing this, the caddie threw the toffee into the zipper compartment of the bag. The result was no more toffee and no more birdies. Then it began to rain. When the golfer went into his bag for a dry glove, out came two gloves, a ball and three tees—all stuck to a large hunk of toffee.

GERMAN CHOCOLATE PIE

Walter Hall

4 ounces German's sweet chocolate

1/4 cup (1/2 stick) butter

1 (12-ounce) can evaporated milk

1 1/2 cups sugar

3 tablespoons cornstarch

1/8 teaspoon salt

2 eggs

1 teaspoon vanilla extract

2 unbaked (9-inch) pie shells

1 cup shredded coconut

1/2 cup chopped pecans

Melt the chocolate and butter in a saucepan over low heat, stirring frequently. Stir in the evaporated milk gradually. Remove from the heat.

Combine the sugar, cornstarch and salt in a bowl. Beat in the eggs and vanilla. Add the chocolate mixture and beat until blended.

Divide equally between the pie shells. Combine the coconut and pecans in a bowl. Sprinkle over the prepared pies. Bake at 375 degrees for 10 minutes. Reduce the heat and bake at 350 degrees for 30 minutes; the filling will set upon cooling.

Serves 12 to 16

THE 19TH HOLE • DESSERTS

FRESH PEACH PIE

Terry Dill

3 to 3$^{1}/_{2}$ cups sliced peeled peaches
1 unbaked (9-inch) pie shell
$^{1}/_{2}$ cup sugar
2 eggs, beaten
$^{1}/_{2}$ cup evaporated milk
2 teaspoons cornstarch
1 teaspoon almond extract

Place the peaches in the pie shell. Combine the sugar, eggs, evaporated milk, cornstarch and almond extract in a bowl and mix well. Pour the sugar mixture over the peaches. Bake at 400 degrees for 10 minutes. Reduce the heat and bake at 350 degrees until set. Cool to room temperature. Serve with vanilla ice cream.

Serves 6 to 8

PECAN PIE

. . . .

Hale Irwin

3 eggs, beaten
1 cup dark corn syrup
3 tablespoons butter, melted
1 teaspoon vanilla extract
$^1/_2$ cup sugar
$^1/_8$ teaspoon salt
1$^3/_4$ to 2 cups pecan halves
1 unbaked (9-inch) pie shell
1 cup whipping cream
1 tablespoon sugar

Combine the eggs, corn syrup, butter, vanilla, sugar and salt in a bowl and mix well. Stir in the pecans. Spoon into the pie shell. Place on the lowest rack of the oven. Bake at 350 degrees for 30 to 45 minutes or until set.

Whip the cream with the sugar in a small bowl. Serve with the pie.

Serves 6

Gayle Nelson found that getting accustomed to Tour life was an adjustment. The 1974 Western Open was at Butler National Golf Club, which was all male, so the facilities provided for the wives were in a small trailer apart from the clubhouse. Larry played well and was in the last group on Sunday. As Gayle tells the story: It was Larry's first year on Tour, and we didn't have much experience playing really late in the last round, so I was a bit nervous. Before heading out to follow Larry, I went to the restroom. Unfortunately, the hostess in the trailer thought everyone was on the course, so she locked up and left, leaving me inside. After expending a great deal of effort trying to open the door, I resorted to banging on the window and calling for help. Sadly, a group gathered to watch the crazy golfer's wife until someone realized the problem. The hostess couldn't be found and no other tournament official had a key to the trailer. After a great deal of time and more attention than I ever wanted, a maintenance man removed the window and lifted me through to applause from the crowd. I caught up with Larry on the second hole.

PUMPKIN CHIFFON PIE

Larry Nelson

1 (15-ounce) can pumpkin

8 ounces marshmallows

1 teaspoon cinnamon

1/4 teaspoon nutmeg

1/4 teaspoon salt

2 egg whites

1 cup whipped topping

1 baked (9-inch) deep-dish pie shell

Combine the pumpkin, marshmallows, cinnamon, nutmeg and salt in a saucepan. Cook over low heat until blended, stirring frequently. Remove from heat and cool to room temperature.

Beat the egg whites in a mixing bowl until soft peaks form. Combine the egg whites, whipped topping and pumpkin mixture and mix well.

Pour into the prepared crust. Chill, covered, for several hours before serving.

Serves 8 to 10

PUMPKIN DREAM PIE

Billy Casper

16 ounces cream cheese, softened

1/4 cup pumpkin

1 teaspoon cinnamon

1/4 teaspoon ground cloves

1/4 teaspoon nutmeg

12 ounces whipped topping

1 1/2 cups confectioners' sugar

1 1/2 teaspoons vanilla extract

1 graham cracker pie shell

whipped topping

Beat the cream cheese in a mixing bowl until light and fluffy. Add the pumpkin, cinnamon, cloves and nutmeg and beat until blended. Add 12 ounces whipped topping and mix well. Beat in the confectioners' sugar and vanilla. Spoon into the pie shell. Top with additional whipped topping. Chill, covered, for 2 hours.

You may sprinkle crushed gingersnaps over the top of the pie if desired or make a pie shell using crushed gingersnaps.

Serves 8 to 10

THE 19TH HOLE • DESSERTS

PERFECT PUMPKIN PIE

Al Kelley

TOPPING
1/2 cup packed light brown sugar
1/2 cup flour
1/4 cup (1/2 stick) butter, chilled
1/4 cup chopped pecans

PIE
1 (15-ounce) can pumpkin
1 (14-ounce) can sweetened condensed milk
2 eggs
1 teaspoon cinnamon
1/2 teaspoon ginger
1/2 teaspoon nutmeg
1/2 teaspoon salt
1 unbaked (9-inch) pie shell

For the topping, combine the brown sugar and flour in a bowl and mix well. Cut in the butter until the mixture resembles coarse crumbs. Stir in the pecans.

For the pie, combine the pumpkin, sweetened condensed milk, eggs, cinnamon, ginger, nutmeg and salt in a bowl and beat with a wire whisk until blended. Spoon into the pie shell.

Bake at 425 degrees for 15 minutes. Reduce the heat and bake at 350 degrees for 30 minutes. Sprinkle with the topping. Bake an additional 10 minutes or until a knife inserted 1 inch from the edge comes out clean. Cool to room temperature.

Serves 6 to 8

FILLED PASTRY SHELLS

Tom Watson

PASTRY SHELLS

$^1/_2$ cup (1 stick) butter, softened
1 tablespoon superfine sugar
2 tablespoons sunflower oil
1 egg, beaten
2 cups cake flour
1 teaspoon baking powder
$^1/_8$ teaspoon salt

FILLING

2 cups milk
$1^1/_2$ tablespoons butter
$^1/_2$ cup sugar
2 egg yolks
2 tablespoons flour
1 tablespoon cornstarch
milk
1 to $1^1/_2$ teaspoons vanilla extract
cinnamon

For the shells, cream the butter and sugar in a mixing bowl until light and fluffy. Add the sunflower oil and egg and mix well.

Sift the flour, baking powder and salt together. Add to the creamed mixture and mix well. Press over the bottoms and up the sides of four 4-inch tart pans. Bake at 375 degrees for 15 minutes.

For the filling, bring 2 cups milk and butter to a boil in a saucepan, stirring frequently. Combine the sugar and egg yolks in a bowl and beat until blended. Blend the flour and cornstarch with a small amount of milk. Add to the egg mixture. Stir into the milk mixture. Cook for 5 minutes or until thickened, stirring constantly. Remove from the heat. Stir in the vanilla. Spoon into the baked shells. Sprinkle with the cinnamon.

Serves 4

THE 19TH HOLE • DESSERTS

METRIC EQUIVALENTS

Some golfers on the SENIOR TOUR are from countries that use the metric system. The following chart will enable American cooks to convert their recipes to approximate equivalents.

PRODUCT	1 CUP	1 TBSP	1 OZ	1 LB
BUTTER	150 G	15 G	25 G	500 G
CREAM	300 ML	20 G	25 G	500 G
FLOUR	125 G	25 G	25 G	500 G
MEAT	–	–	–	500 G
OIL	250 ML	25 G	–	–
SALT	250 G	30 G	25 G	500 G
SUGAR	200 G	25 G	25 G	500 G
WATER	250 ML	20 G	–	–
WINE	250 ML	–	–	–

When approximate conversions are not accurate enough, use these formulas to convert measures from one system to another.

MEASUREMENTS	FORMULAS
OUNCES TO GRAMS:	# OUNCES $\times$ 28.3 = # GRAMS
GRAMS TO OUNCES:	# GRAMS $\times$ 0.035 = # OUNCES
POUNDS TO GRAMS:	# POUNDS $\times$ 453.6 = # GRAMS
POUNDS TO KILOGRAMS	# POUNDS $\times$ 0.45 = # KILOGRAMS
OUNCES TO MILLILITERS:	# OUNCES $\times$ 30 = # MILLILITERS
CUPS TO LITERS:	# CUPS $\times$ 0.24 = # LITERS

PLAYER INDEX

PLAYER INDEX

PLAYER INDEX

PLAYER INDEX

PLAYER INDEX

RECIPE INDEX

RECIPE INDEX

RECIPE INDEX

RECIPE INDEX

RECIPE INDEX

RECIPE INDEX

RECIPE INDEX

THESE GUYS ARE GOOD™

THE SENIOR TOUR WIVES COOKBOOK

Senior Tour Wives, Inc.

P.O. Box 323

Ponte Vedra, Florida 32004

Please send _____ copies of THESE GUYS ARE GOOD™ at $34.95 per book $ _____

Florida shipping addresses add 6% sales tax $ _____

Postage and handling at $4.00 per book $ _____

Total $ _____

_____
Name

_____
Street Address

_____
City   State   Zip

_____
Telephone

Please make checks payable to: Senior Tour Wives, Inc.

Photocopies will be accepted.